If you like stories of God's transforming l
you will love this account of one woma
through life. Susie tells it with disa
helpfully recounts the ongoing healing process through her
journal, her conversational walk with the Lord and the
application into life of the truth that she reads in the Bible. You
will hear many other tales of radical change, but this one is
told from the hindsight of several decades and offers hope and
encouragement to all who will persevere as she has done.
Anne Coles, leadership of New Wine, with special responsibility for women

Joyous and heart-breaking. Shocking but inspirational. The
ruthlessly honest, movingly written, self-penned story of
Susie, our lifelong friend, and her journey of struggle,
redemption and hope.
Steve Chalke MBE, Founder, Oasis UK, and Cornelia Chalke

An amazing story of transformation told with honesty and
passion. This book will touch the lives of all who read it and
give hope to those who feel that, because of their past, they
can never be free. Susie is proof that God accepts us as we are
because we are His children, and gives us wings to fly to the
place of freedom He has planned for all of us ... Her story is a
reminder, too, however, that the journey to freedom is not
always easy and that because we are human ... we will
stumble at times ... Susie takes the risk to be vulnerable so that
other people can find hope and value through the love of God.
Maureen Ross (BA Hons), Divisional Family Officer, Salvation Army

This book is refreshingly honest. Susie dares to take the reader
into her world, whether that be the world of drugs or the
struggles of family life. For many years I supervised Susie's
counselling   it this book
opened my  has now. I

521 384 21 8

recognised afresh why she has such understanding of people who are struggling with life's issues and marvel with her at God's amazing grace. She is truly a daughter of the King, and she is able to rejoice in that even when she is 'getting things wrong'. This is a story for Christians and non-Christians to read. It will challenge, inspire and resonate.

Mary Dicker, Senior Counsellor, Fegans Child and Family Care

When Susie first joined the Tunbridge Wells & District Writers' Circle I recognised her talent immediately. On reading *Potholes and Belly-flops* I was moved by her honesty and her willingness to share this with her reader. In her unique and beautiful voice, Susie describes her life, her faith and the challenges she has faced. Even in the shadows there is light and courage. An inspiring read for the real woman of today.

Karen Rollason, Chairwoman, Tunbridge Wells & District Writers' Circle

Susie is my cousin. I love her and have always loved her. There is something of her in something of me – the same quest for something real and reliable; for meaning in life and the meaning of love – nothing else will do, and nothing else does. I loved reading her book; simply and truthfully told, it is easy to read but not an easy subject to write about – I admire her, and always have. Even though I know aspects of this story, I never felt ashamed of her or even disappointed in her. I have simply loved her, as I think God has too. And whilst I do not exactly hold to the beliefs that underpin this book, I do believe in healing and I do believe in Love. I do believe in faithfulness and forgiveness and in redemption and resurrection and in something eternal, and this book is full of that!

Kit Loring, Co Director, Ragamuffin International

Potholes and Belly-flops

Thoughts from a woman who knows!

Susie Flashman Jarvis

instant
apostle

I would like to dedicate this book to my mother, who always loved me, prayed for me and bought me a pressure cooker.

First published in Great Britain in 2013

Instant Apostle
The Hub
3-5 Rickmansworth Road
Watford
Herts
WD18 OGX

British Library Cataloguing-in-Publication Data

A catalogue record for this book is available from the British Library

This book and all other Instant Apostle books are available from Instant Apostle:

Website: www.instantapostle.com
E-mail: info@instantapostle.com

ISBN 978-0-9559135-8-7

Printed in Great Britain

Instant Apostle is a new way of getting ideas flowing, between followers of Jesus, and between those who would like to know more about His Kingdom.

It's not just about books and it's not about a one-way information flow. It's about building a community where ideas are exchanged. Ideas will be expressed at an appropriate length. Some will take the form of books. But in many cases ideas can be expressed more briefly than in a book. Short books, or pamphlets, will be an important part of what we provide. As with pamphlets of old, these are likely to be opinionated, and produced quickly so that the community can discuss them.

Well-known authors are welcome, but we also welcome new writers. We are looking for prophetic voices, authentic and original ideas, produced at any length; quick and relevant, insightful and opinionated. And as the name implies, these will be released very quickly, either as Kindle books or printed texts or both.

Join the community. Get reading, get writing and get discussing!

instant
apostle

Acknowledgements

The journey to write this book has been long and sometimes arduous and I am so grateful to the friends who encouraged me to write in the first place, and thus enabled me to make my story my offering to God.

So thank you Ali and Gillian Jones, and Steve Chalke, who were in the front line when the internet did its damage and helped to staunch the flow by inviting me to write.

My husband David has always been a solid rock alongside me, supporting me in all I have done, protecting and believing in me. I love you with all my heart.

To my children Bonnie, Millie, Hollie and Lewis – I am so grateful to God for you; you have blessed my life to overflowing, your love and support is amazing.

This book has involved an army of people, because as you will find out I need lots of feedback. So, thank you Sarah, Rhoda, Karen, Carol, Liz and Dilys for continuing to check on my progress.

Cornie Chalke, I will be forever thankful that you read my original first draft years before and encouraged and supported me to pursue my goal.

Karen Rollason, I am so pleased to have found you again and I am indebted to you for your belief in my ability to write.

Thanks to Lyndsey Dodd for giving me your time with such kindness and insight.

For my many family and friends who have loved me and prayed for me through my life, I am forever grateful.

Finally I want to thank Manoj Raithatha and Instant Apostle Publishing for believing in me. I can still recall the day that Cathy Wield, who read it first, called me to say she loved it: thank you for all your support on the journey. I am astounded at the care I have received from the team: Nigel Freeman and Nicki Copeland, your attention to detail are second to none, and this book would be the lesser without your editing finesse.

David Salmon @breathecreative, thank you for designing the cover, for your amazing encouragement as we debated the best way to cover the story, literally.

I am astounded at the way God has provided for me during this journey, enabling me, finally to let go of the reins and to rest in my heavenly Father.

Praise be to God who turns our mourning into songs of praise.

Contents

Author's note

This book is written for all those women and men who have been abused and harmed, for those who believe they are in some way or other too bad, too dirty, too guilty to ever experience the love of God.

He loves you already and just waits to wrap His 'everlasting arms' around you and to call you daughters and sons of the king.

Foreword

'Do you relate to someone in the Bible?' asks Susie Flashman Jarvis in her book, *Potholes and Belly-flops*. 'I do,' she says. 'One is Peter for his charging about way of doing things and the other is Mary Magdalene because of her previous life.'

With honesty and openness, Susie shares her life story; the broken relationships, wrong life choices, family crises, parenting problems, sickness and her long and difficult journey to 'Relinquish control to God'. She talks without concealment of the Mary Magdalene phase of her life, meeting God, the Peter phase of her life and all the problems it brought and her longing to reach a phase of her life where, like the Apostle John, she knows with all certainty she is 'loved in a lavish way...'

This is a real story of a real woman with real issues arising from a wounded inner child, but one who is determined to hold on to the Lord and face the issues, one by one, with courage and dedication.

We all have potholes and belly-flops along the journey of our lives, but not all of us are brave enough to share them openly with the world to encourage others on the same road.

Susie shares her battles with pain, illness, depression, fear, despair and doubt, but also the moments of light, love, grace and blessing when God broke through into her circumstances.

Susie writes, 'The Father is sitting in a room in our lives, a fire is blazing, a seat is pulled up next to Him ready for us to come and sit on and we keep walking by the open door.' Like all of us, many times Susie kept walking by that open door without going inside to sit and rest awhile. When she made a deliberate choice to go and sit with the Father, no matter how difficult the circumstances in her life, work and family, she

began to discover what it is to make a decision to live 'as a daughter of the King.'
Jennifer Rees Larcombe, Beauty from Ashes

The beginning

He sat on the bed. His large bloated body seemed to fill the room.

'If you can find a vein you can have some,' he muttered.

Minutes before I had been sitting in his front room with all those other now nameless faces waiting, hoping for anything going in the drugs department. His slim, almost waif-like, wife busied herself with her children's care and ignored the hurting people who waited. I was one of them – I used my charms to wheedle and whine to get what I needed. How she put up with him and us is beyond me, but I suppose the luxury of hindsight and the knowledge that I now have of women who are trapped in situations goes some way to explaining it.

So he told me, 'I want a hit; you can have some if you can find a vein for me!'

Ugh, how terrible, but I had no money and so no choice.

He immediately removed his shirt as we entered his bedroom and he sat there like a Buddha. His body, bloated from years of abuse, was pale, the skin dull and without the normal lustre you would expect. He was only in his twenties.

'They're all done in, but you might find one in my chest.'

Breathing in deeply, I put my hands on his skin, feeling for that slight rise in the surface that might indicate a vein that could ensure entrance of the drugs that he and I craved.

How have I sunk so low? My thoughts echoed in my ears. I continued to feel the clammy chest that seemed to be craving of its own volition the drug that was needed to assuage the sweats that were starting to plague him.

Suddenly I found a vein and he handed me a syringe full of dark brown fluid. Slowly I inserted the needle and let the liquid enter his body.

***

Throughout life we are assailed by voices that try to direct our steps; voices of those who care for us and those who don't; voices that want the very best for us and those that want to harm us; those that encourage us and those that are jealous of us; those that believe in us and those that are too scared to even hope that we would rise to the challenge and raise our game.

This is the story of one woman who has challenged those inner voices; it is the story of how she still struggles to silence them and how she has discovered the secret of embracing her wounded inner child.

This story begins with the past rising up when life appears to be calm. It starts when someone finds topless photographs on the internet, pictures of me – young, beautiful, troubled me. It starts as I imagine 'dirty old men' pawing over these images and as I feel totally impotent to protect my young form from such affronts. It starts as I fall once again into a mental pit of darkness and shame. It starts as rage once again covers my shame in a defensive mask that I use so liberally. It starts as I talk with friends about how I cannot remove these images but how I could move on, and also with the suggestion that I tell my story; maybe it would not be a waste of time after all, and God would have the victory!

Written over five years, this book tells the story of the road less travelled as I start to understand my past and attempt to live as a 'daughter of the King'.

Chapter 1
Early days

I think I was special then. Mum told me that Dad had danced down the road when I was born, both he and Grandad. I was born in a maternity hospital: Annie McCall's, a beautiful place with green walls and green chintz curtains in Stockwell. At 9lbs 5oz I was the biggest baby girl who had ever been born there. The usual practice then was for babies to be taken to the nursery while their mothers rested. Not so for me; I was a contented baby who never cried and who was never hungry so I was kept with my mother. My mum brought me home to our beautiful flat as a partly bottle-fed baby, but she persevered and I was totally breastfed in the end.

We lived for the first five years of my life in a flat in Peckham with high ceilings and big windows. I can still recall the yellow, grey and white tiles on the kitchen floor. The swirling of Auntie's blue and white polka dot skirt that made a swishing sound as she walked still echoes in that memory; skirts then were full and dropped to the calf.

My parents were Christians and went to Chatsworth Baptist Church in South Norwood twice each Sunday by bus. The evening service would culminate with high tea at Nanny and Grandad's house – my dad's parents. My father was totally smitten with me at the time and would run up the stairs eager to see me. I was only 18 months old when my mother became pregnant with my brother, and she would sometimes rest while my dad and I caught the bus to church. Mum told me the other day how she used to watch from the upstairs window as we walked across the road to the bus stop.

Wearing my little navy blue skirt and white socks and shoes, I would stop and wave to her.

The flat in Peckham had a really long garden with rose bushes running down each side; my brother and I loved it. I think life was pretty idyllic then; my grandparents (my mum's parents) lived nearby in Camberwell Green and we would see them often.

My father and I have a very difficult relationship. I often argued with him about many issues, but recently I had one of those very rare treasured moments where I laid aside my fear and spoke to him calmly, without getting dragged into an emotional interchange. He talked to me about his memories of me sitting with him on the bus, wearing a little checked skirt, and he told me how much he loved me. I was gobsmacked! We all need to find those diamonds in the dust, moments to help us manage life, don't you think? I felt great for days; he had listened to some difficult truths from me and had not knocked me down!

I loved Camberwell Green with its children's 'umbrella' roundabout – one of those tall circular roundabouts that really looked like an umbrella without the material over the spokes; it rotated from a circular point and was a thrill to be pushed round on. Camberwell had some curious shops, one of which was a toy shop. The entire window was crammed top to bottom with dolls and toys of various types. It was like Aladdin's cave. There were also fabulous London markets with men and women shouting out, selling their wares of fruit and vegetables, crockery and clothes; a wonderful rich hubbub of life in all its variety.

My grandparents lived on the Glebe estate in Bentley House on the first floor. There was a tall, walled balcony that ran along to the front door, with shiny red bricks topping it off and from the gaps in the wall I could see the tall tree that sat in an area where cars were parked and children played. One of the people who parked their cars there was my Uncle Len, my mother's younger and wilder brother, who always had a flashy car on the go. I remember his wife Sue with her back-combed hair and heavy black eyeliner and mascara; I would sit on the bed watching as she got ready to go out.

When I think of Nan and Grandad's flat, I think of food: bread and butter, Yorkshire pudding with sultanas, cakes, and warmth and busyness; we would have Sunday lunch with us kids sitting on the curved arms of the sofa in the front room as there were not enough chairs. They had lovely dining room chairs with a pattern carved into the top of them; these same chairs now sit in my kitchen and my children use them.

I loved them both so much; Grandad loved to bet on the horses and kept lots of small biros (perfect for children's hands) and a myriad of betting slips in a drawer in the sideboard in the front room. Drinking glasses of various shapes and sizes were there as well. It was a treasure trove for children; we all had our favourites. The trifle bowl was kept there too, although it was often full and then would be given pride of place on the table.

They also had a mysterious box that held cigarette cards. Some were made of silk; others were black and white glossy photographs with dogs and cats on them, or soldiers. My brother Andrew, who was born two years after me, and I loved to flick them against the balcony wall in our own little game. Grandad smoked Senior Service, with the sailor on the box. I loved the look of the box, and maybe that is why as an adult I loved the look of Camel cigarettes.

Grandad was a real Londoner who would tell us we were 'silly moos' and would pour his tea into his saucer to drink. He wore a white silk scarf, overcoat and a cap. He would always buy *The Sun* newspaper; little did I know then that I would grace its pages one day!

Nanny made me laugh and was so kind; she had the smoothest, softest skin even though her joints were misshapen with arthritis. She would wear those copper bangles to try and help the swelling; I don't recall her complaining though. She had terrible bunions that must have been painful, and swollen ankles as well. In the end she was really crippled by arthritis.

When I was five, my parents, like many people at that time, moved out of London to a new estate that was being built in Kent, in search of a better standard of living. The estates were in the process of being built, and there were vast piles of yellow, clay-laden mud everywhere. It was very difficult for my mother as she was leaving the love and care of her own mother who lived nearby and was moving to a place where she knew no one. She was also pregnant with my sister Mandy.

I can remember my sister's birth. I sat outside the bedroom door on a paisley-covered chair waiting for her to be born. It was a strange time for me because I was about to start school, which meant my new sister and my brother, Andrew, who I was very close to, would be at home without me.

I have spoken to my mum about the birth, but she seemed to think I was outdoors playing. I 'm not sure she would have been particularly aware of where I was, though; I mean, her attention would have been focused somewhere else, wouldn't it?

Chapter 2
School days

I hated my first day at school. I tried to run away. I can still recall the sound of pounding feet as I was pursued by my teacher Mrs Fidget; she wore a tweed suit and a skirt with box pleats. Her big calves with brown brogues completed the image. She finally cornered me in a dead-end corridor.

We sat in our classroom on little wooden chairs with curved backs, and a little boy wet himself; it ran all over the floor. A rather inauspicious start! But worst of all, my brother and sister were at home with my mum.

Life continued and my mother tried to manage with three children under the age of five. I remember that during the holidays the doctor advised my mother to put me and my brother to bed in the daytime for a nap in order to have some rest. She was very tired managing three small children. Life had been difficult just before Mandy was born. Mum had fallen down the stairs and then Mandy was discovered to be breach, so Mum was admitted to hospital in order for Mandy to be turned. It was a successful turn and she stayed the correct way up, or should I say the correct way down!

I recall with fondness those afternoon naps where I would sneak into my brother's room and play cowboys and Indians with small moulded figures. He would be in bed under his candlewick quilt, and his legs would form mountains and hills on which we would stage our battles. The afternoon sun would attempt to burn though the curtains as we waited to be able to get up again. I assume Mum and Mandy would be sleeping all the time we were playing, and we were allowed to get up again once they were sorted.

Life continued. Families moved onto the estate as more and more houses were built, including Rosemary and Roy with their two children, Alison and Timothy. We were soon to become firm friends. Our parents were inseparable and so the two families were flung together. Aunty Rosemary was a musician who taught piano and violin to local kids, me included. I was, just as I am now, an ill-disciplined individual who did not practise enough. Still, I joined the local orchestra playing the violin. I have forgotten everything now, though, apart from the basic ability to read music, which helps my musicality as I sing. Aunty Rosemary would sometimes drive me in her funny little black car which was like a black bubble; its more formal name was the Austin A30. I loved that car; it was a bit like her – unique and round and friendly.

I would run down our street to Aunty Rosemary's house holding my very old-fashioned violin case (I always hated that case), trying to get to the next lamp post before a car came down our road. I really thought that something would happen if the car passed first. I think I was showing traits of OCD – a precursor of my later addictive behaviour.

I was enrolled in ballet classes that my mother took me to on the bus; all three kids and pushchair – my mum was a bit of a star really. Mrs Fox, the ballet teacher, had a tightly pulled-back bun which gave her face a rather stern look, but I remember her with affection as there was always a twinkle in her eyes, and I do recall doing at least one show. During this time Mum met other women who became lifelong friends to her and their children friends to me.

A new addition to our family was Anna. She arrived in a brown cardboard box, a lovely golden bundle of cross Labrador 'wriggliness' who, as time went by, would escape and terrorise people in the road, chasing unsuspecting children. A few years ago I met one of those children who told me how afraid they had all been of her. It's a strange thought that she was allowed to get out because, as a dog owner, I would not allow it to happen today.

(Here is a present-day comment: my dog Solomon went missing not long ago and I hadn't even noticed; he had wandered off when I was emptying the bins and was found and eventually brought home. Oops!)

My sister Mandy was growing up, and I had to allow her to play with me. I really didn't like it; she cramped my style and would get me in trouble.

'I'm going to tell of Mummy,' she would sing.

So I would bang her head on the wall.

We shared a room with a little dressing table standing between our two beds. There was no heating upstairs in our house and I remember Jack Frost would visit, as we would call the ice on the inside of our windows. It was so cold that I would bring all my school clothes under the blankets with me and wait for them to warm up, and then get dressed under there as well.

It's funny how children, me included, recall their childhoods by accessing sensory memories. The cold in the bedroom reminds me of the lounge where we had an open fire which was fired up by a wonderful thing called a gas poker. I loved that fireplace: it was where we would come into from playing in the snow, and put our ice-caked mittens to melt and drip off the fire guard, and where I would warm my frozen feet. I think that maybe my terrible chilblains developed there. It was thought that rapidly heated feet could cause chilblains.I suffered with these so badly that they would bleed as I scratched them with violence in order to relieve the incessant itching. Eventually I was prescribed calcium vials which I had to drink; they were disgusting and I don't think they made any difference – I still scratched.

When children don't have lots of entertainment such as televisions and films they amuse themselves; hours were spent playing off ground 'he' – the name used then for 'it' – and we would climb along the landing using the bookcase where the 'secret' book was kept, trying to keep our feet off the ground as we pursued each other from bedroom to bedroom. The 'secret book' was one that we were not allowed to look at. It was called *Family of Man* and was a book of black and white photographs from an exhibition in New York in the sixties; it portrayed life in all its richness and all its poverty. With its pictures of birth and death, I loved it, and would sneak peeks at it when I thought no one was looking; I love photographs and I wonder if my fascination of the art form is in some way rooted in that book.

The other game that was such fun was spaceships, which we played under the G Plan dining room table. We would pull the chairs in close and soar to planets around the universe. The brass discs on the underside of the table used to cover the screws that attached the legs to the table were amazing controls.

But, to our great excitement, a television did eventually arrive; a grey box with a kind of plastic coating that looked like it had material pressed in it. So we moved on from 'Listen with mother' to *Watch with Mother*. I loved it; *The Wooden Tops* and *Rag, Tag and Bobtail* which, incidentally, I thought were real animals that lived in a wood. It was only as an adult that I discovered that they were finger puppets.

Animal Magic, Daktari, Z cars, Dixon of Dock Green and *The Newcomers* (an early soap) were all sent to thrill us, and thrill us they did.

*****

School life improved over time with lots of good friends. Real fun was had in the playground with kiss chase around the huts and games of marbles in the little circular drains. It's funny how valuable marbles became; I love them to this day, the colour and the feel of them. And jacks; I never did master juggling those funny metal shapes on the back of my hand and then bouncing the ball and scooping up the rest of them. Then there were the handstands against the wall with our dresses falling down over our faces, ensuring that our navy blue knickers were on display. French skipping with elastic wrapped around our ankles became all the rage as well as clapping. I really don't remember any bad stuff from that time. That came later.

It was around this time that I got my two mice. One had a short tail – I chose him deliberately. His name was Stumpy (unique, eh?). I had gone to my friend Alison's house to discover that her mouse had had babies, and there were loads of them. Well, I had to have some! So I found an old fish tank in the garage and took it upstairs and hid it under my bed. I found an empty jam jar and put some cotton wool in it. I really don't know how I managed to get it upstairs without my mum finding out. I brought the two mice home and would bring them out at night to run over the bed covers. I even recall taking them to school; I honestly don't know how I did that. I would cart them around in my pockets, it felt exciting and risky.

Then the inevitable day dawned when Aunty Rosemary had a conversation with my mum. I was summoned downstairs and asked, 'Do you have mice in your bedroom?' I retreated upstairs and brought them down in their bed – the jam jar! Mum was horrified and informed me that she would have to tell Dad. The picture that stays in my memory is my mum leaning on our white upright piano saying to Dad on the telephone, 'Susan has been keeping mice in her room.'

I waited for his response, almost holding my breath, unsure of which way it would go. When the sound of his laughter echoed down the line from London, I was so relieved. In many ways it was typical of my dad: he encouraged the extraordinary things in life but was a complete pain about the mundane not coming up to scratch.

Chapter 3
Teenage years

One day my parents threw a big party for my dad's work friends; I can recall vol-au-vents and various other delicacies and my mum's famous choux pastry éclairs. This was where I first experienced a snowball – a delicious mix of vodka, Advocaat, lime and lemonade, so yummy; a lady gave me one in an eye-winking sneaky fashion. The ladies wore stilettos, wrecking our parquet wooden floors, but fun was had by all.

Food featured loudly in my growing up, whether we had lots of money or not. Mum made delicious tea loaves that we would spread with butter and eat for Sunday night tea. Bananas and custard, curries with lots of trimmings, hidden delights like sultanas and banana that my childish palate would relish. I would love sitting there with all the little dishes laid out in front of us: yogurts and chutneys and meat and rice. Crumpets dripping with butter and large oranges that Mum would peel with the juice running all over her hands. Dad would slice fruit and place it enticingly in front of him: pears that he liked when they were still hard, and apples – we would all clamour to get some. Sometimes as he ate his lunch I would watch him; he hated his lunch plate to be piled too high and would shout at Mum, demanding that she take some off, but when she did he would eat in a particular way, saving some of everything until last. It would make my mouth water as he added extra salt and pepper to his last roast potato and wiped up the remains of his gravy.

Christmas in our house was so exciting; we each were given one of my mum's stockings – real ones, old ones with ladders in them. We would place them on the ends of our beds and wake to long, deformed, knobbly leg-like structures stuffed with a satsuma wrapped in foil, nuts, a kaleidoscope and small toys of various sorts. Christmas morning was presents around the tree from Mum and Dad, parcels beautifully wrapped that intrigued us as we guessed what was inside. Dad always made a lot of effort wrapping presents; I remember him teaching me how to fold over the corners and make them neat. Funny really, those things used to matter to me, and I do appreciate them, but they don't mean the same any more.

Easter was a time of traditional breakfast. A couple of years running Dad painted the eggs: he was an artist and would go to a great deal of trouble to paint our faces onto our boiled eggs, which made them too good to eat. So we would keep them until they went off. Of course, we kids would scoff our chocolate eggs quickly, but Dad would secrete his away and produce it one evening weeks after Easter as we watched TV. He would break one half into pieces and place it in the other half of the shell and would offer it around to all of us.

***

The other family who were important to me were my father's parents and my cousins. Nanny and Grandad lived on the Isle of Sheppey. I loved going to see them. They lived in a bungalow that Grandad had built himself. It was full of brass ornaments and Toby Jugs that we would make up imaginary games with. There was a large back garden with secret places that we could hide in, and Laddie their Collie dog was there, like a large black and white shaggy moving rug.

Mum would pile us kids in the car and collect Dad from the station. We would then drive over to visit our grandparents and Dad would eat the casserole that Mum had made for him, while Mum drove. Uncle Roy had taught Mum to drive and she had eventually passed her test on the fourth attempt.

My grandparents were Christians. It is my belief that their prayers and the prayers of my parents kept me from an early death or from a deadly illness.

They attended a little corrugated iron church that was full of ladies in hats and smartly dressed old gentlemen; women whose voices warbled as they sang the old songs, 'Tell me the old, old story of Jesus' love for me'. I would try to contain my laughter and not to catch the eye of my Nan, who would close one eye as she laughed and shook.

Grandad was a deacon there and highly respected. My father's brothers, Uncle Steve and Uncle Colin, lived there too. I imagine that they were about to leave home; Uncle Colin, tall and lanky, would walk me around the garden as I stood on his feet. Uncle Steve was a guitarist and would play songs. I loved him: he showed me how cool God was and how believing in Him was the best thing.

The other family that was part of the fabric of my life was my father's sister and her husband – Auntie Kathy and Uncle Al – and their children – Carol, Keith, James and Jo – my cousins. Boxing Day was always spent with them; a feast of wrapping paper flying around the room and presents opened with noisy excitement, and mountains of food piled onto our plates. Memories of playing murder in the dark and the squeak of the metal horse that rose and fell on four springs and a rather bedraggled dog on wheels warm my heart. These people continued to love me through the very dark days of my life, and still do to this day.

Life continued, marked out for me by my brother's train tracks; the transformer would often go wrong and the trains were tricky little things to get on the tracks, and the tracks themselves were a pain as well. We would sit on the parquet floor in the front room with it all laid out, arguing about who was going to turn the dial. It gave off a smell that my husband says was electrical burning.

My father built me a dolls' house (I still have it; my children played with it and I hope that my grandchildren will do the same) and my brother had a fort for all his cowboys and soldiers. A Sindy and Patch doll were my pride and joy. Patch was Sindy's little sister who was a tomboy and had a short brown bob with a fringe. I loved her best because she was like me – naughty. I didn't have much furniture but I had a wardrobe for them that would easily be transformed into a boat or a car. We did not have a lot of money but I loved the dolls that I had.

It was here that I first loved the underdog, or those seen as unlovely. I had a big doll called Caroline. She was an ugly doll who looked as though someone had stood on her face, but I loved her even though I apparently pulled out her eyelashes because I thought they would grow back.

At the age of nine I contracted jaundice. I was off sick from my primary school for a long time. I remember the day I became ill. I was making my bed, it was a bed that I loved – it had a wooden headboard and I felt very grown up having it.

That day, I was pulling up the bedclothes – I also had a candlewick quilt; I used to love pulling out the strands – and I just laid my head down. I was standing at the time but I just couldn't move. My mum was shouting for me and I could hear her voice but I was unable to respond. I was aware of her in the room trying to get me to speak and move but I couldn't do anything. It was so bizarre. So I was absent from school for a long time. My mum, who was very good at doing that mothering thing, used to make clothes for my dolls and leave them on my bed to find in the morning when I awoke.

When I eventually returned to school, the teachers told my parents that there was nothing they could do for me; I think they were implying that I was stupid or something. My mum has recently thrown more light on the subject by telling me that they had said I would have to be put in the bottom class as I had missed so much school – I had been absent for a month or so. My dad was having none of it, so my parents put me in a little private school, a train ride and walk and trolley bus ride away.

I loved it at Shernold School. I had elocution lessons, not that you would believe it now! This little school was wonderful for fishing for sticklebacks and playing 'sardines'. As I think of that I can almost smell the apples that were rotting around on the ground near the barn that we would cram inside. A cidery, not particularly nice, smell, but one that brings a smile to my face as I think about it. It was an idyllic environment, with no health and safety – wonderful. Grey felt hats and straw boaters and walls that surrounded a small garden. I climbed those walls every day for a week and every day I fell off. Today I still bear a lovely little scar on my knee that I had to cover up when I used to do modelling.

Everything about this school was an adventure. Some things I liked; others I didn't. Take the train journey, for example. There would be 'the green boys' to mess about with on the train; boys who wore tempting green caps and blazers whom we would tease. In those days there were individual carriages as well as larger ones, some with luggage racks made of knotted string. We had great fun climbing up into them and would spend the journey there. We would cross the road and wait for the trolley bus once we arrived at Maidstone station and listen with our heads against a post for advance warning of its arrival.

One of my not-so-nice memories of the train journey was one return trip when we were sitting in a railway carriage opposite a man who stared at us as he clenched and unclenched his hands. It was very frightening. Suddenly Alison, my friend, saw someone that she knew; the lady was getting out at the next stop and said that she would drive us both to our station. The only trouble was that I did not know the woman and I had been taught not to take lifts from strangers. So Alison got out and I refused, and I stayed on the train. I moved down the carriage and spent a scary 15 minutes until I reached my stop. Still, I survived and lived to tell the tale. Our journeys to and from school continued for two years until I reached the age of 11 when I had to change and go to a secondary school.

The school my parents sent me to next was the school that followed on from my previous primary school. It was getting the best O level results at the time and so it appeared to be the best choice, although it did not turn out that way. Age 11 found me a skinny and not very attractive child: I have seen the school picture and I seem to recall that I was all teeth and eyes. It was hoped that with my new uniform I would fit into the school with ease. But that was a joke.

There I was, skinny and small and speaking very nicely. I could recite 'Cats sleep anywhere, any table, any chair, top of piano, window ledge, in the middle, on the edge' with perfect pronunciation. It was not looking good. Now add into the mix the old-fashioned skirt; box pleats were in, with wide waistbands, and skirts were short, but I had to wear one with concertina pleats an inch wide with a very narrow waistband and it came down to the knee. I looked like one of those old-fashioned lampstands.

But kids are resilient, aren't they? I started to fit in by learning how to speak slang and dropping my t's and not watching my p's and q's either. I got on with the so-called 'lower classes' and they were very kind to me – they did not seem to mind my uniform, which was such a relief. In fact, it was here that I developed the practice of stopping fights and trying to prevent trouble. 'Poking my nose in' is what my husband calls it, but I just can't stand injustice, and today I champion the cause of the undermined, whether they are male or female, child or old person. Being a counsellor enables me to support those who feel worthless and facilitate them in a process of change – a massive privilege.

My years in that school were fairly troubled; I was picked on, bullied really. My father had proved them wrong: I was put in the top class, but it was here that I was not accepted; it was here that I encountered some of the girls from my previous primary school. I feel rather bad writing about it as one of the instigators has apologised to me and we are friends now. But I suppose facts are facts, and it did impact the way I think now.

I was slow to develop physically, and it was really terrible when everyone else was wearing a bra. Let me tell you, friendships were made and broken on whether or not you wore one. I recall a drawing of a stick person – me – that was sent around the school by someone. It had arrows that pointed to two areas and said 'flats to let' and 'land for tropical development'. It was terrible, I was mortified, and the boys saw it! My mum took me out and bought me a bra, size 28 – two flat triangles – but it was better than nothing at all.

I have a memory of my friends playing 'taming of the shrew', and I was the shrew. We wore grey, thick stockings and suspenders. I had a really pretty suspender and I was so proud of it – it had little flowers on it. One day they thought it would be funny to rip the stockings off and throw my shoe out of the first floor window. Not a very nice experience.

But things started to change when one day I encountered one of the girls alone and she started to bang my head on a brick wall. I just looked at her until she crumbled before me and begged me not to tell my mum. I discovered then that the best way was not to react.

But I was still desperate to fit in so I became class clown and started to get into all sorts of trouble. I discovered how much I had tried to fit in about 15 years ago when I was running a pre-school. Picture this: one of the ladies who worked in my pre-school had gone to the same school as me and said to me one day that I used to pick on her in the school canteen with all the other girls. I felt so ashamed. I don't think it got any worse than that, but that was bad enough. I counsel children in school now who have to put up with that sort of thing, and it is terrible.

Anyway, I started to grow taller and I grew six inches in a year. I am now five feet and eight inches, or should I say I am when I wake up, but by the end of the day I seem to lose an inch.

So there I was, taller and starting to feel better. Boys were starting to notice me – a very important thing – and then one day a cookery teacher, for some unknown reason, informed me that I had hips like a carthorse. That throwaway comment has forever affected the way I look at myself; it's ridiculous I know, but it is true. I see in the mirror a narrow set of shoulders with wide carthorse hips slung underneath. It sounds like I have Body Dysmorphia, but I don't, just a bad, on occasions, body image. I can't believe what young girls have to live up to now with all the computer-enhanced images that are bandied about in all the magazines.

Chapter 4
Sex and drugs

Drugs began to feature in my life during my teenage years. The first joint stays in my memory – unlike my first sexual encounter!

My friend and I had bought ourselves some grass which we took to a five-bar gate overlooking a field on the pretence of walking her dog, and we rolled the fattest joint imaginable and smoked and coughed over it together.

So my drugs journey had started just up from the parade of shops where we would steal our lunch. We really didn't need to – we all had pink dinner tickets that we had bought with our parents' money but somehow it was more fun to pinch it. I think we were bored, a bit over-the-top, middle class kids with nothing better to do with ourselves. For me that joint was the beginning of a slippery slope that quickly moved through the normal route, as it was then, of speed and acid (LSD). The acid part of my life should have been a warning to me as hallucinations and weird happenings invaded my mind, but I suppose I must have been unhappy because I didn't stop.

Home life was a bit stressful, to say the least, and I made pathetic attempts to leave home, once coming back for my hamster and another time my mum found me and got me home by saying that if Dad found out he would lose it. And, having always been my mother's defender, I came home.

So like I said, I became more physically mature, but with that maturity did not come emotional maturity. I would play about with various boys, allowing them to touch me sexually outside the back of the halls where the discos were held; my father would collect me afterwards, totally unaware of what I had been up to. My parents were much stricter than my friends' parents and would insist on collecting me. I thought it was a pain, but my friend told me that at least it showed they cared.

All my friends had lost their virginity by their sixteenth birthday and so, after going out with someone for a year, I finally had sex. I remember calling up my friend to say that I had finally done it. I don't remember the act itself, only a sense of achievement in having finally plucked up the courage to do it.

One time I had taken LSD and it was Sunday. I rang my parents to say that I was not going to come home.

'Oh yes you are,' was their response.

I had to go home, and the drug was just starting to take effect. I arrived home unsure how I was going to survive lunch. By that time we had moved to a big Victorian house with massive rooms and tall ceilings and I found my brother in the dining room.

'I am on acid,' I told him, trying to explain what was happening.

He didn't have a clue what I was talking about. I sat through lunch trying to eat food that tasted like cotton wool, feeling like everything was going in slow motion. I was hallucinating; the faces of my family were distorting before my eyes. My parents were mad at me and I was trying to act normally. I have no idea what they thought.

My life at home started to be very turbulent during those teenage years. My parents' marriage had always been volatile, with Mum trying to keep the peace. My dad was a smoker then, and through my early years I remember being sent round the shops to buy Gold Leaf cigarettes for him, which he would then go and smoke on the toilet. It was in these local shops that I started to steal the odd bar of chocolate while I was getting the cigarettes. Dad was a nightmare to be around if he ran out; in fact, Mum says she put them on her shopping list to prevent him blowing his top. We all walked on eggshells; I preferred to walk to school rather than get a lift with him and then have to put up with his anger at other drivers. Or I would ride my Raleigh bike, one with small white wheels and a large white pannier on the back loaded with books, but at least it was peaceful.

All through this time I was going to church, and I did in fact believe in Jesus, but I found it hard to fit in. I have amazing warm feelings towards the ladies who faithfully taught Sunday school each week. I really loved them.

While I was a teenager I became like a lot of kids that age – a bit mouthy with big opinions. The one thing I hated was hypocrisy, and I thought that my father was a hypocrite. As I have already mentioned, he was really mean to Mum, and I couldn't stand it. This eventually resulted in physical assaults from my dad towards me. He bought me a book on a couple of occasions by way of apology; one was a book about the painter Constable. I don't remember him actually saying sorry as such, but he would write things like 'just a token' in the inside cover. Those beatings had a detrimental effect on my brother and sister but I was unaware that they knew about them at the time. It is only in recent years that they have told me how they heard what was going on from outside the bedroom door.

I felt absolutely alone.

Through these years my Christian faith did grow, and I would go and stay with my aunt and uncle who were only a few years older than me. I even had a Christian boyfriend, although I was already walking a sexual path and tried to persuade him to do likewise, but he was having none of it.

I so wanted the faith they had so I would try and pray out loud but would feel so stupid and my heart would be racing in anxiety as I worried about saying the wrong thing. I did not know then what I know now – that God sees our heart and is not worried about the way we say things. We are, after all, talking to Him, not to people.

I started to lose my way. My mother had prayed with us kids each night; she would stand out on the landing with our bedroom doors open so we could all hear her. But that was before we moved to the big house where everything went wrong. If a child sees faith enacted in a cruel way, they start to question the truth of it all.

***

I did rather badly in my exams, but after retakes I finally got a few O Levels and so was allowed to stay on to sixth form. But I was bored and left before my time and then tried college.

I also dropped out of college and started working in a day-care nursery; I remember earning £10 a week. I continued in this job until I went to Canterbury to start nursing training. I had an older boyfriend at that time who took me to Paris one weekend. To be honest he nearly slipped my mind when I was writing this book, which is almost a foretaste of all that was to come.

The nursing was a mixture of pain and pleasure. I made really nice friends there but a sister in charge of the ward that I worked on was very unkind. Needless to say, I did not last long in nursing, but it was not my fault this time.

I suffer with hypermobility (not that I knew that then) and I fell on my first attempt at ice skating on one of my days off and dislocated my kneecap, which resulted in me being unable to walk for a while, thus missing an important ward in my training. I had spent three months on the male geriatric ward and was due to go on male surgical but this was not to be. I needed an operation to correct my kneecap, and as I was training as a nurse I was moved up the waiting list, but I did not have the operation in the end as I did not go back. This meant that I ended up living at home again; not a good idea when I did not get on with my dad.

Chapter 5
The hippy trail

The change began, I suppose, after I left school. While in school I did take rather a lot of recreational drugs, but none of my friends ended up like me. I was rebellious in nature and, although I don't hold my father responsible, I do think that if you grow up with anger and distrust, with that constant 'walking on eggshells' thing, it does affect a young developing mind. I work with teenagers now and I see it all the time.

I grew up angry with my dad because he was often unkind, but then he would confuse me because sometimes he was really nice. But he seemed to always mock my mum, or to think he was better somehow. He was the man who played King Crimson during Sunday lunch (a supposedly cool thing to do in those days), but it was to my mum I would talk rather than to him, not that I told her much either. I was angry with her, too, because she let him be so powerful. Still, I would always defend her, even to the present day.

The saddest fact really is that my dad did love us and he did take us to church, and he was a Christian – a man of passion – but he appeared to be lost in a sea of anger and resentment.

So anger and drugs, anger and drink – yes, I believe they go together.

We all need to feel important, and I think that is in part what drove me to seek relationships with men. I think I needed a relationship that would value me for me, but instead what I found was that, in the main, it was my body – the way I looked – that was most important to men, and so I used it.

It is so sad to think that I did that. I remember being told by a friend that the guy I was going out with was only going out with me because I looked good; I think I was 15 at the time. I have never forgotten that. I wanted to be wanted for all of me, when really it is natural to be attracted by someone's looks as well as their personality. So I took it badly. It is rather confusing, to say the least: I am a typical woman who thinks about what she looks like and takes care to a certain degree, but I still struggle to believe that other people think I look good. The people that I value in life I love because of who they are, not what they look like – caring spiritual men and women full wisdom and love. They come in all shapes and sizes; some are into fashion and some are not bothered. But I want to be valued for who I am regardless of how I look.

So drugs – how did I get so hooked on the hard drug scene? I said before that I needed to be loved by someone, and there was someone who I thought was so good looking, and he was older than me and taking heroin. He introduced me to the stuff. I don't think either he or I thought it would lead to a problem, but it did for both of us.

Drugs seemed to infiltrate my life at an alarming speed. I work time out by remembering who I was living with at the time. My twenties were punctuated by a successful modelling career and a series of live-in relationships that each lasted about two years. The first relationship, from the age of 19 to 21, involved drugs and an overland trip to India. I was a grafter even then, and I funded our trip by working cleaning toilets.

The trip involved us hitchhiking through Europe. We got a lift in Austria from a kind couple who took us to the house that they were going to stay in for their holiday. There we were treated very well – we were fed good food, we slept in clean beds and generally had a great time. When we were ready to move on they took us to the nearest main road so that we could continue our journey. I have under my bed in an old photo album a picture of me looking like an old lady with a head scarf on; I thought I was so cool.

So the journey continued with sleeping in office block doorways and waking in the morning to find people stepping over us in order to go to work.

It was in Yugoslavia, as it was called at the time, that we experienced some trouble. It involved me nearly being sexually assaulted by a Yugoslavian lorry driver whom I fought off in silence while my boyfriend slept in the cab next to me. It was far too risky to shout out at the time as my boyfriend had a knife, and I was scared someone might have got stabbed. I recall wrestling with this man in the darkness; as I think about what a close shave that was, I am aware that God must have looked after me!

My boyfriend was rather surprised when I asked the driver to drop us off at the first opportunity the following morning, and I was relieved that I had kept the incident to myself as he was rather het up about it when I told him what happened.

It's funny, really, that any man was interested in me, as I had had a friend cut off all my hair before we even left England. I had heard that it could be very difficult for Western women in some of the countries we were going to visit and I was determined not to do anything to provoke the men (this was the age of bra-free hippy women wandering around Muslim countries and being surprised that they were attracting negative attention!). I was determined that I was not going to be like them so I suppose I was hoping I would pass as a boy. No such luck.

We went down to Athens where we picked up the Magic Bus to India! This took us up to Turkey, and Istanbul, a place of cafés and the Blue Mosque. It had dark streets and brightly lit cafés with old men smoking hookahs – brass pipes with up to four long bendy pipes attached that different people used together. You would light the tobacco and hashish and the

42

water in the lower chamber would bubble as you sucked on the pipe; we called them hubble bubble pipes.

Iran and the city of Tehran came next, and the scary experience of men who would try and touch me. The majority of the women wore traditional clothing that hid them from the eyes of men, so to have lots of scantily dressed girls wandering around was too much. I, however, was covered.

Two men, my boyfriend and another man, would walk with me in an attempt to protect me, but a few hands got through. It was a pity because it formed a negative view of the place in my mind, and now I suppose I am still biased and would be anxious today at the thought of going back.

As we travelled across the country, we experienced hostility in various villages; people would throw rocks at our coach as we drove hurriedly through.

It was in Iran that I first experienced opium – wads of thick, gooey stuff that was smoked. It was horrible stuff, with all the images of sordid opium dens truly attached to the drug itself. It seemed to have an almost sordid effect on the mind, with a nauseous side effect.

Afghanistan was my favourite country on that journey. It was here that we purchased Ritalin (known today to help ADHD sufferers). We bought it over the counter from pharmacies; we had some sort of story about why we needed it, but I really don't know how we even knew about it. It was like taking speed and so would balance out the very heavy black resinous hashish that we smoked. What a crazy way to live, to smoke something that wipes you out and then to take something to restore some sort of normality. It begs the question, why did we bother to take anything at all? Until I started to write about this travelling experience, I really believed that I did not have a drug problem at that time; looks like I was wrong!

Afghanistan was such a beautiful country and Herāt was my favourite place, with lovely streets with white buildings and the Green Hotel with an oversized chess board in the garden. I am so pleased that I experienced it before all the wars overtook it. It was here that we received a letter from my dad that asked my boyfriend to look after me; recognition at last!

Pakistan was our next port of call. It's funny, I don't seem to remember much of the place but I do recall a rather heavy border with a museum that displayed the various ways they had caught people trying to smuggle drugs through. I was going to put a slab of black hashish inside a Nivea tin, but I am so glad I changed my mind (maybe God helped me) because they dug out the cream!

The one thing that I remembered last night about Pakistan was the big, overcrowded, brightly coloured buses strewn in flags and bright lights and absolutely covered in bags and people of all shapes and sizes. It was these buses that we passed as we wove our way over the difficult winding mountainous roads that were the Khyber Pass. As I remember these buses, I can almost hear them erupting with music and noise, but then again maybe that is colour that my memory has added to these images. I think the main sound I recall as I dig deep in the recesses of my mind is the sounding of horns, horns of greeting and horns to say move out of the way. It is a wonderful memory, full of life and with a complete mix of feelings: fear combined with excitement and expectation as we journeyed ever nearer to India.

Finally we arrived at our destination: Delhi. We were the lucky ones as, while still on our way there, the whole coach load of us had been asleep and someone had broken into the bus and stolen loads of belongings. I was sleeping with our passports and money inside my sleeping bag, but they managed to steal many passports and lots of belongings and money from fellow travellers. They even lifted my legs off my bag and rummaged through that. Just shows how easy it was to rob drugged out and exhausted travellers.

Oh how I love India to this day – the people and the sights and sounds, the colours and the bustle. We made friends with a group of Sikhs who ran a taxi company, I don't know how we got to know them but we used to eat breakfast with them. They probably bought it for us as I do recall money was getting rather tight. They thought it was hysterical if they could manage to smuggle a chilli into my omelette sandwich, but I still remember their kindness with warmth. They even drove us south to Agra to see the Taj Mahal: it was so beautiful. I don't know why they did it; they certainly got nothing in return apart from our company.

I also had my first experience of 'Delhi belly' here; suffice to say that I did not leave the hotel room for days. My boyfriend went out scouring the markets for the best deals on bananas to bind me up. When I was eventually able to leave the room, we came back one day to find a wall had turned black, but it was not until closely inspected that we realised that it was moving and was covered in ants. I freaked out and demanded a new room, which they obliged us with.

Delhi is a city of markets with brightly coloured saris and mounds of sweets: sticky and wonderful. It is also a city of terrible poverty where children are maimed in order to make them more adept at begging. I can recall children pulling themselves along on little trolleys inches off the ground or just sitting there in pitiable silence. I have since learned that gangs often ran the beggars and so they did not receive what you gave them anyway. It is a city of heat where the air is thick with fumes and noise of motor rickshaws ducking here and there and weaving in and out of the traffic; they were such fun to ride in.

I don't know how long we stayed in that city, but lack of money forced our return. We did not have enough to pay for both of our fares homes so we looked for another way and found it when my boyfriend offered to drive a coach back to England. Now God must have had a hand in this as well: the man who owned the bus wanted it taken back to a village only about ten miles from where we lived in England – we could not believe it! My boyfriend did have a licence, but not one for driving a bus, and a wreck of a bus at that. There was no heating or screen demister which, it turned out, would be very necessary on our journey home.

So we set off from India with only a few passengers. I don't recall the reason – maybe people weren't travelling then as they knew that the weather was going to be really bad. My memory of the journey is very hazy, with vague images of deserts and cold – unrelenting cold. As I have already said, there was no heating so my boyfriend drove with his body in a sleeping bag; I really can't believe he did that, but I suppose he had no choice.

Picture this: there we were, him driving and me holding one of those flame thrower things aimed towards the windscreen as an attempt to remove the ice and mist. How crazy can you get?

Driving through a desert – I think it was in Iran in the middle of the night – we suddenly hit something. We clambered out of the bus and there, swaying on its four legs, was a donkey. It was bizarre – he just stood there. We could do nothing and so we just got back on board and carefully continued on our way.

It was in a city somewhere that the diesel froze in the tank of the bus. I think the temperature was something like 30 degrees below (that would be in old money – remember I am of the generation that knows it's hot when the weather man says it will be over 70 degrees) so it was cold enough! My feet became blue and I can recall a group of people finding a bowl of warm water to put them in, an attempt to restore circulation. It was night time and while I sat with my feet in a bowl someone lit something under the bus to try and melt the diesel so that we could continue.

Honestly, it sounds totally mad to me as I remember, but I think when you are young you just get on with things; it is only as you get older that you fear your own mortality and take risk assessments. The rest of our journey back through Europe must have been relatively uneventful as I don't remember it at all, but I do know that on our return we both slept solidly for two days and nights!

What a journey! That felt like a bit of a marathon, and as I write I have been asking myself, 'Where was God in all of that?' Apart from the obvious times I have mentioned, He must have been in the rest of the journey, for He knows me, He made me and He knows what I am going to do as well as what I am going to say before I even think it! And yet, mystery of mysteries, He still loves me and, of course, you as well.

Chapter 6
Model days

How did I move from a young woman of 19 with a bad homemade short haircut into a Page Three girl? The journey began on my return from India when I started work in a Job Centre in a local town. The idea of a Job Centre was a new concept and they were trying to advertise the facility. I was asked by a photographer to stand in for a photograph and I obliged. I then seized the moment and asked him if he would take some pictures of me so that I could try and get some modelling work. He immediately agreed but suggested that I borrow a wig!

I really should have known better because when we arrived on location for the shoot he suggested I pose topless. I really don't know why I went along with it; maybe I thought I would have to do that in order to be a success. I was selling myself short once again. How often do we do that? How often do I do that? It's like we don't really believe we are worth that much, but God knows better and loves us with an inexhaustible love that stretches to encompass us. He sees all that we are and all that we can become. He is the perfect parent!

The photographs were so amateur: a young girl wearing a ridiculous wig that was so obvious – you know, one of those ones where the hair has a nylon look to it. And standing by a gate or sitting there half naked. I don't know why I did it. I also wonder at the kind of man he was to suggest it.

I'm not a shy person; I had been sunbathing topless for many years, but to appear in a national paper is another thing. Anyway I took the pictures to London. I'd never been there on my own before – how funny is that? – I had travelled all the way to India yet going to London was rather daunting.

I had rung an agent, Tom Sheridan at International Models, who had asked me to come and see him. I recall walking into his office while he was on the phone to someone and hearing him say that a model with an incredibly long neck had just walked in and would he (the person on the phone) like to see me? It turned out that he had been talking to *The Sun* newspaper's main photographer, Beverly Goodway. My feet did not touch the ground. Within something like a week I was in the paper. For some reason I was a great success, which I enjoyed, but of course it was all about the way I looked, and so my focus on what I looked like continued.

This was also a difficult time for me because my Grandad, who read *The Sun* every day, rang my parents and announced in his proud voice, 'Hey, our Sue's in the paper!' My parents were mortified whilst he, an avid *The Sun* reader, thought it was amazing.

It was rather strange because I must have mentioned this to one of the photographers, and before I knew it there was the story in the *Daily Mirror*. The trouble with being caught up in the business is that nothing remains private, and so every opportunity was used to reveal details of my life to the public. I was very young, and when I think back to that time I am embarrassed that I allowed them to take advantage of me to that extent.

I had been baptised when I was 17 but my faith was borrowed from my parents. It is very hard for churches to hold on to young people who get caught up in the world and all its distraction, and I was no exception.

My father never took kindly to being told what to do with regard to himself or his kids. There had been some sort of breakdown in my father's relationship with our church. I am not entirely sure what happened but I think he would have become defensive when they mentioned my work; mainly getting my breasts out in national papers! What I really needed was someone to come alongside me; I don't know if I would have taken any notice though. Writing this is spurring me on to get in touch with my youth leader of the time to see if she remembers what happened. I will start with my mum first; she will probably be able to fill me in.

I asked Mum what happened and she told me that someone in the church had visited my dad because I had become the forces mascot as a Page Three girl. How about that! I had no idea; I could not have remembered that without her help – I bet she has a picture somewhere to prove it! The church did not approve of a baptised believer doing such a thing. I can't blame them really: it's not what Jesus would have encouraged me to do.

I identify with the Samaritan woman at the well, ostracised by the people but not by Jesus. She became, after Jesus had challenged her, the woman who went away and told everyone what Jesus had said. I suppose I am like that: I am the woman I am today because of what He did for me and I want people to know that so that they can be encouraged and know that they are never too far from God's reach.

I had really wandered away from the church and was starting to earn real money. I had my first job abroad for a German magazine. Would you believe it, it was a two-week trip to the Maldives, but it was topless work and we stayed on a nudist island. The photographer and his two old assistants were not a pretty sight to behold!

One day I stood all morning in the Indian Ocean, topless and holding a reflector board (a silver board that reflects the light and takes away the shadows on the face). At the end of the day, when I started to take off my make-up, I discovered a massive fluid-filled blister that covered my cheeks! It was really bad and I was unable to work, so I just had to sit in the shade wearing an enormous hat waiting for it to go down.

I did manage to swim amongst the atolls a couple of times though, and it was a beautiful place. It was here that I learned to play backgammon, and it was also here that I began a period of unfaithful behaviour. I do feel a sense of shame as I recall how I behaved, but I know I am not that same young woman any more. God has changed my heart and, amazingly, my mind as well. I often work with people who suffer with anxiety and I talk with them about capturing their thoughts. I would love to quote Scripture to them but it is not my place as a therapist. If I could, I would quote this:

We demolish arguments and every pretension that sets itself up against the knowledge of God, and we take captive every thought to make it obedient to Christ.
2 Corinthians 10:5

If I, we, could live like this we would live freer lives. We would know our value in God as precious sons and daughters of the King, and as such we would not let ourselves be fooled into listening to lies about us, portrayed in the obscure expectations of others.

The only real way to enable change to occur is to relinquish control into the hands of God, so really it's about obedience and not trying to do things alone, which is rather a hard thing for a strong, independent woman like me.

Back in England, I was modelling and trying to live an idyllic life: my boyfriend and I rented a rather nice bungalow on a farm. We grew vegetables and tried to live a romantic, self-sufficient life, but it didn't last and we moved to a lovely wooden chalet in the woods in the grounds of a big house. I was supposed to clean the big house for a few hours so that we could live rent free.

Now cleaning was never my strong point... I can hear hoots of laughter from my friends. I remember dropping furniture polish through the strings of the grand piano!

Thankfully they allowed us to increase the rent, and were probably relieved that I was not cleaning their home any more. I'm not sure who was more relieved – them or me! As a result, and because I was still working as a topless model, I was photographed for the newspapers once again as they invaded my private life. This time it was a double-page spread which described me as a topless Mrs Mopp, and even I was embarrassed at that! Would I never learn?

Chapter 7
The slippery slope

My relationship ended and I moved on to the next relationship and on in my modelling career. I stopped taking my clothes off after finally listening to some good advice and I found myself a new agent. My career was going great guns; I was the first 'Impulse girl': 'Men just can't help acting on Impulse!' And I was shooting commercials for television for various other good products after becoming a favourite of one director. One was filmed in the ski resort Val d'Isère and involved me pretending I was older as you needed to be a certain age to advertise cigarettes. Another commercial for Harmony hairspray was filmed alongside Lesley Ash, who was young enough at the time to need a chaperone. We filmed the commercial in San Diego Zoo, and it was a really fun-filled time.

I was delighted when I went to Leicester Square to watch a film and suddenly my face filled the screen wearing a De Beers diamond ring. I so enjoyed shooting the commercial: Tony Scott was the director and I had to go for the casting with lots of actresses and actors. I was thrilled when I got the job. My on-screen partner was Peter Duncan of *Blue Peter* fame. Really I wanted to do more acting, but for some reason I got more involved in the drug scene.

In contrast to my successful career was a private life that was starting to be dominated by more and more drugs, including the use of heroin. My boyfriend and I would have violent arguments which would result in me throwing things. He had a volatile temper, too, and we would scream at each other. I think our relationship was based on insecurity. I was

53

always worried that he might go off with someone, and in return he was jealous. We lived in various flats around London, and heroin and cocaine became evermore regular features.

We continued to live together and people in the modelling world were starting to get worried for me. While shooting the Impulse commercial my boyfriend called and demanded that I went home. The team thought I should stay with them as it was a two-day shoot, but I didn't. Stupid really. I don't know why I was so naive. He was not working and I was earning all the money, so why was he so powerful? I did love him, but it was ruined by drugs and the fact that God was not in it.

We later moved to Amsterdam and lived there for about six months. Once again I was successful in my work, but my agency was concerned about my relationship. Drugs were involved and I recall a raid by the police: we were both asleep and they barged in through the door. Police in Amsterdam carry guns, and my boyfriend had a knife, so I jumped on the policeman's back and hung around his neck. I can't believe they didn't arrest me!

Once again, the contrast in my life was extreme: drugs on the one hand and luxurious trips abroad and expensive clothes and food on the other; big posters displaying my face one day, sniffing heroin and freebasing coke the next. It was a very surreal existence. There were good times in it, but the memories are full of drugs and extreme behaviour. I was, of course, unfaithful to this boyfriend too, which was quite surprising because of all the men I had relationships with, he was the one I really cared about. But I was on a slippery slope, and drugs and lust had their grip on me. One day I came home and heard him singing in the shower and I knew he must have found a job – finally – but it was too late for me; he had taken too long. I had been on his case for ages to find work and my patience had finally run out; he had not got his act together in time for me.

I had become involved with a couple who were ten years older than me, spending a lot of time in their home, and so I went to stay with them; they lived what looked like the so-called idyllic life with their little boy. I have memories of him eating Weetabix with yogurt and milk and thinking that she was such a good mother – well, until drugs took their toll on her, too.

Their marriage was collapsing and so I ended up in a relationship with her husband whilst she was seeing someone else. I did have some concern that I had hurried along the end of their relationship, but she never told me that. I don't know why she still loved me, but she always did, and we remained friends to the end of her life, even though I didn't see her for more than a decade while she continued the life of drugs after I had stopped.

I received a phone call out of the blue about two years ago.

'Hello Sooze,' croaked the voice on the end of the phone. 'It's me.'

I was thrilled to hear from her, but she had an agenda in ringing: she had cancer, lung cancer. So I suppose she was ringing to say goodbye. I dropped everything and dashed down to the south west of England. When I arrived I pulled into the car park of a grotty-looking block of flats, and there she stood, the same friend but encased in the body of an old woman. As I walked towards her the years melted away, and we stood with our arms wrapped around each other.

The years of alcoholism and drugs had finally caught up with her; I was overwhelmed with a sense of sadness. But in spite of that she looked after me like she had always done. She had made me a bed even though the bed was broken, so I had to sleep the wrong way up; she washed my jeans and ironed them for me. It was crazy really – she was dying yet looking after me! It was as if the woman from before had become submerged in a world where her essence had trouble in surviving and now, too late, she was surfacing again.

She was still the wonderful funny lady that I had known, but it took her being with me or with people like her lovely son and sister for that creative fighting spirit to surface. I got us an Indian takeaway that evening and she told me how she had become someone who sat on a park bench drinking, how she had no money and couldn't even afford to get a bus into town to get to the hospital: it was tragic. She could barely walk; and the truth was that she didn't have the energy to stand at a bus stop even if she could walk to it. I just could not believe what had happened to her. It was like I was being dunked into the world that I had left so long ago. Poverty was now her enemy, and she had no one nearby to transport her or help her with the everyday problems of survival. All her friends were in the same position as her – addicted to drink and/or drugs. I took her to a supermarket to buy some food; she had never used a debit card, as she no longer had a bank account. Life had moved on without her.

We spent the evening looking at pictures and remembering life before it went seriously wrong: a trip to the south of France where we had stayed on her sister's campsite and had such fun. I remember finding a gold ring buried in the sand, engraved with the words 'Xmas 1887'. It was really beautiful, but like many things, it went missing. It was not a secure world that I inhabited.

We recalled boyfriends and seriously illegal behaviour which somehow we had got away with. It was ridiculous the things we had done; in many ways they were the actions of teenagers, but of course we were adults. She was the most hopeless shoplifter, and if we hadn't been breaking the law our actions would have been comical. She would stuff her jacket with all manner of things and try and leave the shop looking pregnant! If CCTV had been around then we would no doubt have had longer criminal records. There was one occasion when she was caught and taken away to an office. I didn't know what to do, so I waited a while and then went looking for her. When I entered the office she said, 'Hi,' and called me by her name, and I suddenly realised that she was pretending to be me. I can't remember exactly what happened after that, but I know she went to court as me. Somehow the truth must have come out because I didn't get a record for that crime!

It must have been towards the end of our close friendship when her behaviour became a bit crazier and I moved to north London with her ex-husband. With the luxury of hindsight you can see why you make certain decisions or why certain things push you to behave in particular ways. As I think back and try to dig deep to understand, I wonder why I thought it was ok to have a relationship with her husband, for although her marriage was over and she had boyfriends, there is something within me that tells me that I contributed to its closure.

The pictures of me that we spent the evening looking at revealed a very young-looking girl of 23, while her husband was a man of 33. Maybe I was looking for the approval of an older man. I don't know for sure; it just doesn't add up. Or maybe that's been the story of my life: trying to seek the approval of men while finding them lacking – they could not repair my relationship with my father or substitute him. Only God has really provided me with what I need – acceptance and challenge – but always from a position of love. I recognise that my experience of trying to make myself pleasing to men is not mine alone.

Another reason for the relationship was the common denominator: drugs, namely cocaine, and loads of it. My need to feed my habit of one sort or another seemed to dictate my next move and relationship.

I was very sporadic in my contact with my family, as I didn't want to let them see me in a state. One of my cousins, Kit, who is now also a therapist, kept in touch with me. He's a guitarist, and we would sit on the front porch of the house where I lived and write songs and sing together. I loved the fact that he kept in touch with me, that he loved me and wanted to spend time with me. I never felt judged by him, although he would have challenged me about drugs, I'm sure.

This period of time in London was rather confusing because I was really successful in my work but lived another life when I came home. Drugs were never far from my mind: I was either thinking about where I could get them, or stoned from having taken them.

As I picture my life there, I recall shopping in lovely delicatessens and cooking stir-fry in a wok and making soups in my faithful pressure cooker. It was all so ironic: I sought out healthy food whilst taking hard drugs –– maybe I was in some way trying to redress the balance.

On one trip to Italy with my roadie boyfriend, I contracted food poisoning and, while rushing back to England for a job, I was discovered lying on a bench in Milan airport unable to stand. They took me to the airport hospital and then put me on a plane for England. I was met with a wheelchair, taken through customs and placed in a taxi. After being examined at the Royal Free Hospital I was given some sort of chalk-based drink and sent home to shiver in front of my two-bar heater!

During this time, a good friend of ours died when he rode his motorbike under a lorry. It was a tragic accident, and the following day I had a modelling job to do for the album cover for ABC called 'Lexicon of Love'. I don't know how I did it. A vast amount of cocaine and very puffy eyes disguised by foundation was the solution of the moment.

One day my boyfriend came home with the side panel of a bus shelter; on its reverse was a full-size poster of me! It graced the hallway for ages.

There was a lady in London who sold us cocaine: it was through her that I met a very famous singer who I struck up a friendship with. I have a lasting memory of her laying in the bath at the Chelsea Arts Centre and me sitting on the side talking to her. She may have been famous, but she was screwed up just like me and seriously into drugs.

I continued to do really well in my modelling work and went to Japan for more than four months where I was able to earn a lot of money. The relationship back in England continued even though I was away, but I was extremely promiscuous in Japan, and it was during this time that I started to really see myself clearly.

I recall sleeping with many men: Japanese, American, British, it didn't matter. I continued until one day someone used me like I used them. I felt just like a tramp, and I suppose I was one. I have no idea why I was like it out there because I was sharing an apartment with lovely girls who did not behave like me. How mad. I seem to recall that they warned me about my behaviour as well. Why did I seek close encounters? Why did I think I would feel better? I didn't.

I think I was just typical of some people in that drugs world. I thought it was cool and that cocaine was a high-class drug and that it brought some sort of status. What a load of rubbish – it is dirty and leads to debauchery and crime. It's a closed community where different rules apply – no apparent morals (none where I was concerned anyway, it was all about how to get drugs) and a purely self-serving attitude. For me, it was all about how to survive and stop the pain, and that pain could be anything from a difficult childhood to abuse, bereavement, family breakdown, bad self-image, being bullied. You name it; any issue can drive a person to seek solace in a substance that appears to be fun and then turns into a way to prevent the world from being so hard.

When I returned from Japan, I decided that I would buy a flat with the money I had earned. I found a lovely top-floor flat in West Hampstead with views across London. I met the man that was selling it and he wanted a £7,000 deposit. I was advised not to pay it straight to him but I ignored all the advice and he ran off with my money. He just disappeared into thin air! I told you I was impulsive.

I left the UK to accompany my boyfriend to Canada. It was great fun. We then decided that we would go to America. I had filled my passport up so we had to go to Ottawa to get me a new one before they would let me in. We chose to drive a car overland to California; you could use the car for free if you delivered it.

I do recall a romantic moment when my boyfriend stopped the car on a road in New York and disappeared. I sat there getting rather annoyed when there was a tap on the window. He was outside holding a Tiffany box with a beautiful gun metal pen inside. I kept that pen for many years but I don't remember what happened to it. In fact, I had forgotten that he gave it to me until I was talking about my book with a friend of mine. She is my oldest friend (I had better say that I mean we have been friends the longest) and she never forgets anything, thankfully.

We then drove the car across the States to California where we lived for about three months. It was an amazing journey! En route we visited the Grand Canyon, an amazing, breath-taking place.

I was stopped twice by the police for driving too fast. It is crazy really – all those open roads and a big car and a very silly 55 mph speed limit. They were very kind to me, though. On one occasion I had been driving barefooted, which was rather embarrassing when I got out of the car. We used CB radio out there and I used to laugh when I heard the truck drivers comment about a young girl in a Cadillac, but it was very useful when it came to advance warning about police.

I remember pulling into a gas station late one night and refusing to get out of the car because there were hundreds of very large flying bugs that had been attracted to the light. Our windscreen was a regular bloodbath of casualties. We eventually got to Los Angeles in a record three days due to copious amounts of either speed or coke – it usually takes much longer. I was unable to get work, though, as I did not have a permit.

We were not into heroin when we were in America, just cocaine and dope, and I have to say I have fond memories of trying to equip our apartment with various articles from garage sales.

We did have a great deal of fun, but back in England again it all went pear shaped. I was doing well with my modelling work – my pictures graced magazines, television commercials and large poster campaigns. But on my last return from Tokyo (I went there twice) my boyfriend went off on tour to somewhere and I was left looking after his young son whom I had always loved so much. This was at a time when his ex-wife was unable to manage. I actually registered him in a local school where we lived. When I think of the effort I put into my own children it horrifies me to think that I was left in charge of him. I did love him and never put him in any danger, but I am sure he must have seen me stoned on many an occasion. We definitely smoked in front of him, and I don't mean just cigarettes!

So left alone in England I went straight back on heroin, I really don't know why. I had been off all drugs for five months while I was away in Japan, but it was the drug of choice for my group of friends and I just went downhill. I became very manipulative where drugs were concerned; I am sure I just stayed around certain people in order to get the drugs I needed. The only common ground we had was our need for drugs, and this brought a sense of camaraderie, but it was false, and the relationships fell apart really quickly.

Chapter 8
My body is a broken temple

It was around this time that I met the man who would become my first husband. He lived south of the river and ran a market stall and also sold drugs. It was an irresistible combination. I started to help on his market stall. I remember seeing him for the first time; he drove a nice car and dressed well. I was a very manipulative young woman where drugs and men were concerned. I don't want to be too harsh on myself looking back, but drugs really do change a person, and they did that to me.

I experienced him as an elusive man. He had a reputation of being very private and hard to fathom – just the sort of challenge that I liked, and so I worked my sexual power on him. To put it bluntly, I think I wormed my way into his affections. He could have done without me. I would drive across London on the ruse that I was helping him on the stall, but my partner at the time must have realised that I was extricating myself from our relationship and there was nothing he could do to stop me really. So eventually I left and moved in with my new man.

This was not plain sailing as he shared his flat with a couple who were not on drugs and did not approve of me. I managed to stay, though. He was quite a heavy heroin user and sold drugs to maintain his habit, but he was also a hard worker and ran a stall and did building work. I remember him as a fastidious man who took great care of his appearance. How we both deteriorated so fast is hard to imagine, but we did. We sold more and more drugs probably to maintain two habits; I think I was very demanding and greedy. I am recording my worst side here, but I did have some good attributes, such as encouraging him to re-establish contact with his young daughter. In fact, I became very good friends with her mother: it was her flat that I was staying in when I finally experienced the revelation from God!

We were both going downhill rapidly. I have a lasting memory of a friend coming to buy some drugs and keeling over having taken too much. I honestly thought he was going to die and so I had to walk him, and sometimes drag him, round and round the balcony of the block of flats that we were living in. It was awful! He did live, thank goodness.

Meanwhile, the Falklands were invaded and the world continued to turn, and I was still stuck in my own little orbit.

Life continued and we acquired two kittens, Tosh and Tootsie. I loved those cats but I recall a litter tray overflowing with excrement under the kitchen sink – how disgusting. It must have smelt so bad!

How terrible are the effects of drugs: we would steal electricity by bypassing the meter with a wire. I remember the wire catching fire and me trying to dislodge it with a wet toilet brush (God must have wanted me to live). It was a crazy life. I lost more and more weight and slowly the modelling jobs started to disappear, not surprising really. My partner ended up in prison for signing on and running a market stall, and this hurried my demise. I became even more manipulative. He was coming off drugs and I was just taking more.

He eventually came out of prison off drugs, but it didn't take me long to entice him back on them. How awful! I was totally enmeshed in an addictive cycle. I recall selling my possessions for money for drugs. My mum had let me take a lovely vase when I had left home; it lived under my sink when it wasn't used, and you can imagine I didn't get many flowers. The day I took it to an antique dealer in Greenwich stays with me – I felt really ashamed. I knew that my parents really liked it. But the worst of the many things that I lost was the pearl ring that my grandfather had given me. It had belonged to my grandmother. I was desperate for some heroin one night and my giro was not due until the morning. I went round to a local dealer and bartered my ring for a £5 bag of heroin. That night they were busted by the police and I never saw my ring again. I was devastated.

I was rapidly becoming a skinny wreck. I was told that I looked so ill as I shuffled up the hill from our flat to buy the curry sauce and chips that we ate so often.

I found myself pregnant. We made plans for us to marry but I continued to use drugs. Everything was put in place for the wedding. My mum made my dress. I was not at peace though, and then I lost the baby. I was devastated and now didn't know what to do. It had all gone too far, the plans were set and there appeared to be no way out. How my parents managed I have no idea – my sister was also getting married a month before our planned date.

We went ahead. It was all very difficult. For me it passed in a drugged haze. I have a terrible memory of sniffing a line of heroin off the cistern in the church toilets wearing my wedding dress just before I walked down the aisle. As I approached my soon-to-be husband I started to talk to God.

'I'm sorry, I'm sorry, Lord, for what I am about to do.'

It was no good. We were married, and the drug taking continued. We took our wedding-presents home and opened them in the flat. I am pretty sure we didn't have a honeymoon because surely I would remember. What I do remember is having sex on the front room floor of the flat with someone else only 12 days after we were married, for some heroin. How awful. I can really only bear to write this stuff because I know that I am now a new creation. I could not live with myself if I did not know that God loves me. Still, I feel terrible shame at the thought of how I behaved.

I lost another baby later – what chance did a vulnerable foetus have in such a hostile environment that was my body? I remember discovering the loss in the house of a big dealer. His wife was kind to me but I knew it was my fault; I could not change.

My sister had now had her first baby and it was my absolute delight to look after him on various occasions. What struck me then and stays with me to this day is the way she trusted me with him. In spite of my addictive behaviour she still saw the 'me' underneath. She still loved me.

It was around this time that my bad behaviour finally caught up with me. We were raided by the police and they discovered a small quantity of heroin in my bag and some cannabis. I couldn't believe it. We knew that the police were watching our flat and we were in the process of moving, and I had no idea that the heroin was there. The police were very kind to me. I followed them when they went outside and listened as they walked down the stairs. I heard them saying, 'She's a nice girl, I don't know what she's doing there.'

I ran back into the flat and a knock came on the door. One of the policemen was standing there.

'Here you go,' he said, and handed me the cannabis back. 'You might need this.'

So today I still carry a conviction for possession of a Class A drug. I cannot escape it, every time someone carries out an Enhanced CRB Disclosure – the form needed to work with children –the information is passed on. My past is in many ways my present, even though it took place more than 30 years ago and I am now completely clean. I received a year's probation and I still carry the stigma of an ex-user.

God must have been looking after me, though. It's the power of prayer because my grandparents and my mother prayed for me every day of my life. I remember a case where two dealers (a husband and wife who had four adorable young daughters) were busted. They received ten years each and their children were taken into care. I regularly got my drugs from them. Their children were so lovely. The newspaper headline read 'Bag of heroin kept in doll's house'. It was a terrible time; many houses that I went to scoring my drugs had children in them, neglected and vulnerable.

In July 1985 the Live Aid concert was on and I watched it from a bed in south London, taking drugs. I was a heroin addict married to an addict. Life did not look promising. I was unemployed; in fact, I was probably unemployable. In two years God would have turned my life around and I would be in labour waiting for the arrival of my first daughter. But at that moment I had an existence to participate in and I was starting to experience a sense of loss. I had been invited to a party to celebrate the concert at an old friend's house in Tunbridge Wells, but I was a mess and instead stayed in bed.

I was starting to look towards God and took my husband to a church service: it was a very small group of black men and women who sat in a circle taking communion. It was an intimate service and we were welcomed. I don't remember what my husband thought of it, but it does indicate that I was trying to get back to Jesus and a life of faith.

However, I deteriorated and became a more desperate user, constantly going round different people's houses hoping to get some drugs. I did try to regain control by not taking any heroin for two days, and then I would imagine I was in control and start again. I was living a difficult life. All our money went on drugs; we would reuse the cotton wool that was put in the spoon to boil up the heroin. It was used as a filter but we would boil it again to see if we could get any more out of it. We would do the same with cigarettes: dog ends were collected and the tobacco removed and rolled into new ones. It was all pretty disgusting.

Life was hard and people did die, including a lovely young girl who was the mother of two young children, and people became ill. How I escaped HIV is beyond me: we reused and shared needles. We would scrape off the barbs from needles to make them smooth again. It was so sad, what a waste of lives.

The final straw before my experience with God was an incident where I had no money and was practically begging various dealers for some drugs. There was a dealer out on a housing estate in Woolwich who was a powerful individual with lots of flunkies to do his bidding, and their payment was heroin. He was married to a slender young woman who did not take drugs, and they had a young child. How she put up with all the people in their flat is beyond me. I suppose that is what happens when you are with an addict and stuck in a cycle where the money needed to survive comes from an illegal source: you have to put up with the punters. It makes me shudder to recall this as I type. I did find a vein, as I said at the beginning of the book, and he did give me some heroin, but for me that was as low as I was prepared to go. I was overcome with shame and I felt like a prostitute: even though I had not slept with him, I was going into his bedroom and providing a service for him. In many ways it marked the turnaround, and I finally moved towards a change.

Chapter 9
Freedom

I often tried to go more than two days without drugs but would usually fail. On one occasion I was staying with my friend when I pulled a Bible off the bookcase beside her bed. She was not a Christian but she did have a vague faith in God, and for some reason I had given her the Bible. I did what I have so often done in my life, opened up the Bible in a random way to see what it says. As I started to read, the room seemed to go white and a hushed silence fell on it.

It had opened on Psalm 32:

> What happiness for those whose guilt has been forgiven! What joys when sins are covered over! ... All day and night your hand was heavy on me. My strength evaporated like water on a sunny day until I finally admitted all my sins to you and stopped trying to hide them.
> *verses 1, 4, 5 (Living Bible translation)*

Oh my goodness, that's me, I thought. I could not believe it. As I read on I realised that there was only one way out. I prayed to God and asked for His help, realising that I could not do it on my own.

In a throwaway comment my friend said, 'If I could have the physical pain then you would only have to deal with the mental stuff.' God must have been listening because I did not have any withdrawals but she suffered with flu-like symptoms. It was a miracle, and I did not take heroin again.

I left London and went back to Tunbridge Wells and stayed on my parents' sofa. That didn't last long, as you can imagine. I was still smoking and behaving in an inappropriate way and I couldn't stand it there. They probably had done nothing wrong and had put up with a lot from me. Imagine my visits home over the years: I was either being a very successful model coming home after various jobs abroad looking all tanned and lovely, or I was a wreck, nodding off at the table because I was so heavily under the influence of drugs. I smoked constantly and had permanently yellow fingers from the nicotine. I actually remember using a pumice stone on them to try and rid myself of the disgusting stain. I must have smelt really bad; I know I hate the smell of cigarette smoke now, let alone the breath of a smoker. When my husband used to smoke I would tell him that he had grave breath!

I must have been difficult to be around, but some old friends who had never taken hard drugs came up trumps and put me up on their sofa, which was so kind of them. They helped me to find a flat, but I then continued my promiscuous life, running two relationships at the same time. I was still not able to extricate myself from a sexually available way of thinking. I can't believe the liberal way that I gave my body away.

It was at this time that someone got out a Ouija board and I participated in a session. It was absolutely terrifying. The glass moved under my finger with a life of its own and told me that it saw my behaviour. I was mortified; I thought it was going to say out loud the antics that I had been up to: two men at the same time, etc. I was really aware of dark spiritual powers, and although I had done terrible things before, I had never seen spiritual darkness in that way. It was like Satan's darkness was resonating with my darkness and saying it had common ground in me.

I was used to sitting in God's love even though I had walked away, so it was not good discovering that maybe I had more in common with the devil! I was being seen for what I was: not a very nice person really, and I have to say that I don't know what those men saw in me, or maybe I do – free sex.

At this time I recall thinking I was pregnant and considering fleeing back to see my husband in London and him offering to take me back and raise the child as his own, what a lovely thing to say. I was not pregnant, however, so I did not go back. I think I caused him a lot of unnecessary heartache. I really was selfish, and I am sorry.

Chapter 10
A new life

I was still unemployed until my friend whose sofa I was sleeping on and who had found me a flat also got me a job stuffing envelopes. It was while I was working in this courier company full of very hairy, leather-clad bikers that I met David.

How the mighty have fallen, I thought, as I sat in the back room of the office stuffing envelopes. A quick trip out of the room resulted in me squeezing past a tall, tanned, good-looking man. I looked up and thought, wow, he's nice. And he was: he was known as a really nice guy, too. So that was that; in my determined fashion I set out to get him. I have to say I don't remember if he asked me out or vice versa, but I would not have put it past me asking him!

So we ended up on a date, and true to my way of behaving we slept together on the first night.

He was really lovely, but there were things about him that, well, if not annoyed me then maybe they confounded me. He had his own bedsit that he had bought! But he slept on a very uncomfortable fold-out bed settee and had posters of topless girls lounging around on motorbikes on the walls. He dried his clothes by draping them over the back of horrid plastic/leather-look armchairs and lived on Fray Bentos pies and chips (he had the nickname of Tramp because he would eat anything) and he was not a Christian (not that it seemed to matter then).

We were in some ways a bit of an odd couple: he was a biker and so had lots of biker friends; I had never hung about with bikers. In fact, I had not been on a bike since I was a teenager. I was an ex-heroin addict with a very dodgy past and he was a lovely salt-of-the-earth guy who had lived with his parents and saved for a flat and had had a couple of serious girlfriends and was just starting to get out there and enjoy himself again when I came along. Poor thing!

I had been going out with other men but when I met David all that changed, I wanted to be with him. In fact, I seem to remember talking to him about another girl who he was thinking about, or had already asked out. I pushed him to choose me, and he did.

A group of his biker friends were going off to France so he asked me to go. I had travelled the world but I had not been away on a motorbike for any distance and the idea was exciting, if not rather scary. So we went off camping in France on the bike with a load of his friends. I can still see my mum's face when we turned up on the bike and told her, 'Hey, Mum, we're going to France on the bike!'

What I put her through beggars belief!

It was a strange time for me in many ways because I really did not know David's friends at all well and I felt like a fish out of water. I really needed David to help me to feel ok, not because I wasn't but because I was insecure. They had a sort of wacky, rude sense of humour that I had not encountered before, and I didn't know how to be around them. But it was fun and we got there and back in one piece. I was so relaxed on the way back that I fell asleep on the back of the bike and David had to keep banging his helmet on mine to nudge me awake. I think that was when I realised that he was an unusual man, in that he would keep me safe.

So I continued going out with David; he either stayed at my flat or we stayed at his. And then the inevitable happened: I fell pregnant. Well, of course, I was absolutely thrilled at my unexpected surprise; the question was how to tell David? All I remember was saying to him that I was going to keep the baby whether he stayed with me or not. I did add a rather foolish subclause that having a baby would not affect us! Little did I know!

He did not want to have a baby yet or be married, but he stayed with me, although we did not get married: we had only been together a few months, after all. He said it wasn't anything to do with me but he just did not want to be married. I feel compassion towards him as I write this, but at the time I felt really insecure, despite my bravado.

I moved into his flat and we decided that we would buy a house together. His parents were wonderful; it felt like they loved me as soon as they met me. I immediately felt part of the family.

It was about that time that I went back to church. My sister took me to the Baptist church which, would you believe it, just happened to be two doors down from David's flat. I walked in as a pregnant, unmarried woman and was really welcomed.

It's strange really, because the people who welcomed me were not at all like me. I thought of myself as a rebellious woman whom people would find rather extreme, but these people were so lovely. Barbara, with her hair swept back into a bun, alongside her husband Les, would open the double doors and motion me to enter the church, smiling and loving. I would then sit behind an older married couple called Joyce and Robert; she shook when she spoke and Robert sang with a deep baritone voice. I was greatly impressed by his love for her. They would always turn to me and ask me how I was. It was truly lovely. I have to say that without them I probably wouldn't be where I am today, and they didn't know the impact that they were having on me.

So there I was, about to have a baby, going to church but still smoking dope. (I can hear you gasp, still smoking cannabis while pregnant!) Well, I did say that it was a journey.

Back to pregnancy and life with David: living in his bachelor pad was a squeeze. It was very small and we had to sleep on a sofa that literally folded out in half, producing a rather uncomfortable still slightly folded surface that ensured that you rolled in towards each other, and it had a wooden edge that ran the entire length. The naked girls on the walls upset me, but who was I to comment, having once been a poster girl myself, and my picture probably adorned other men's walls! But comment I did!

I was still trying to behave as if being pregnant made no difference! David had just discovered the joys of doing whatever he felt like; he had only had his flat for 18 months when I turned up. Talk about cramping his style. But he still wanted to be with me and was very kind, really listening to me going on and on about what stage I was at in the pregnancy, how big the baby was, etc.

Both of us were driving huge distances, me in a van (promoted from stuffing envelopes) and him on a bike. We would return in the evening absolutely exhausted with the sensation of either car or bike vibrations still coursing through our bodies. Life seemed to be moving on at a rate of knots; the more the pregnancy progressed the more urgent it became to move into another place.

David may have been a typical biker but he was one who had his wits about him, and he owned his flat, as I have already said. He had lived at home while he saved up (I told you his parents were great) and so now we were in a position to look for a house. His flat had increased in value substantially but still it only enabled us to look for the tiniest of houses: two up two down, front door leading directly into front room, probably terraced, plus we needed space to park his bike. The hunt was on.

We looked at so many places; all of them felt too small (to me). Until one day I found what I thought was an ideal property. It was not terraced, it had side access for the bike and a haphazard lean-to structure, perfect for doing bike repairs, down the end of the garden. The only trouble was that we were not ready to move in yet, plus we had to persuade the mortgage company that we could afford it and I had to persuade David (which was a very close run thing).

Before we moved, David surprised me by buying me a car! I came home one day, to him saying, 'I have bought you a car.' I couldn't believe it: no one had ever done that for me. He pointed to it through the window of the flat. My eyes scanned the car park. Was it that big one there, or that other one? 'It's the yellow one,' he said, and there was the smallest car I had ever seen, a Fiat 500. 'I got it for fifty quid,' he said. I was both thrilled and disappointed all at the same time. But I'll tell you what, I loved that little car. I would pile my other now pregnant friends into it, a bit of a squeeze (a bit like the joke, how many elephants can you get into a car?) and we would bomb about all over the place. It was the first of many yellow cars that we owned, all costing next to nothing.

Stan and Jean, who owned the house we wanted, were brilliant. They really wanted us to have their home. They had lived there all their married life. Their adult daughter and her family lived next door so it was important that they liked the people who moved in. So they waited for us and eventually, when I was six months pregnant, we moved in. We couldn't believe it – rooms, and lots of them. We were thrilled, if not a little stressed at the prospect of paying for it (especially David).

I was now more pregnant, tired and irritable. I was becoming more insecure as the days went on. I had my name on the mortgage – security that David allowed me. He was lovely to me but I was jealous about all his friends, male and female, who came round to our house. I would lie in bed listening to them partying downstairs; I am not sure why I did not join in, apart from being too tired. But I would lie there imagining all sorts of inappropriate behaviour going on and every now and then I would barge the front room door open and glare at them all. I suppose they thought I was one seriously hormonal woman, which of course I was.

One day I felt the first pangs of labour, and off we went in my little car, bouncing down the road. But I was a novice, labour hadn't really started yet. Ugh, we were in for the long haul. We paced around the hospital for hours, the TENS machine strapped to me, trying to counteract the pain, to no avail. Eventually our beautiful daughter emerged into the world. We were both overwhelmed. Everything seemed to fit into place, and breastfeeding came naturally. In fact, I recall a nurse talking to a new mum about feeding her baby and mentioning the various ways to hold the baby while you did – on your side, baby on a pillow, or like Susie...

In those days (a phrase that makes me sound like someone out of the ark) they kept you in hospital for five days for your first baby. This was a good thing in some ways, but I got bored and resorted to smoking dope out on the fire escape of the ward (it horrifies me now to think what I was like, so selfish). Lots of people came to visit me to keep me company. They would all bring toys; there was only just room for Bonnie to fit in the cot as there were so many. I was really exhausted but I didn't listen to advice and the guests continued to arrive. One very welcome guest was my brother who brought pink champagne. He was moving out to America that very week, so a bittersweet memory as now we do not see each other enough.

Chapter 11
We are married

The day arrived to take my clean, white, pure, unsullied daughter home. We got home and I placed her car seat on the chair and gazed about in shock. David must have had a wetting the baby's head party the previous night and forgotten to clear all the beers away and had just given them a cursory shove under the coffee table. It is one of those things that drives me crazy about the lovely man I married – he is messy (not that I am really tidy!!!).

So baby made three and I tried to fit her in with the way of life of a childless couple. One memory will always stay in my mind: all the lads had decided that they were going to the beach for a party and we (well, David) wanted to go too. I was in a quandary as I was insanely jealous and insecure, but I wanted to be a good mum as well.

So off we went in our funny little Fiat 500 and everyone else on motorbikes! When we got there we placed our daughter in her Moses basket next to us on the sand and the party commenced. I turned to look at Bonnie asleep to discover that someone had emptied their shoe of sand over her face: she was sound asleep with her eyes full up! I was absolutely horrified and freaked out, as you can imagine. She was absolutely fine, but did develop an early case of conjunctivitis! I was beginning to learn that babies do change your life, and so was David.

One change I experienced was that I wanted to keep Bonnie near me, but we needed me to earn money. So I started working as a childminder. Now that is one job that is seriously underrated. Imagine the responsibility: someone else's much-prized offspring is placed in your care What a privilege. What a lot of work! Bonnie was still a baby and I was looking after other babies as well. I feel tired at the thought now.

Eventually an ad appeared in the local paper asking for someone to look after two young girls aged three years and six months. Bonnie was now nine months old so I applied and started what turned out to be a three-year relationship with a lovely family. I carted these three girls around in my second yellow car – a beat-up estate which one day started to spew smoke from under the bonnet causing me to stop rapidly, place three young children unceremoniously on the pavement and watch the smoke turn into flames. Honestly, there was never a dull moment!

As I previously said, my name was on the mortgage, David had stayed with me and I didn't really think he would leave me. But I did not feel ok. I was now involved in my church and felt very much a part, but I was still an unmarried mother. I wanted to become a member but was unable to. Philip, our lovely minister, told me that he would give me the same pastoral care as anyone else but he could not let me become a member as it would be saying that the church agreed with David and me living together. I was not offended, though; I thought he was right but I was still unable to persuade David, who was not a Christian, to marry me.

Christmas was approaching and David asked me what I wanted. 'A ring,' was my reply.

And that is exactly what he gave me – an engagement-style ring. Did he mean it in that way? I really don't know, but I was so determined. 'When are we getting married?' I asked.

Poor guy, I never gave him the opportunity to ask me himself. I just ploughed right in and took the reins yet again. It is something that I now regret because it took me years to believe that he had really wanted to marry me.

Something else was going on at this time. I was walking closer with God and so I started to listen to him. 'He will not marry you until you stop smoking.' The words were loud and clear.

I didn't have a problem with God telling me things, so I stopped smoking cigarettes that January and smoked my last joint in the April (I am aware it had taken me a long time to do this!). In the August we were married.

Bonnie, then aged two, was my bridesmaid, my parents bought my lovely dress, a friend provided the food (I am not sure if I really thanked her enough – it was a feast!), others helped decorate the hall and my pastor married us.

Bonnie had an ear infection and screamed the church down: my poor sister had to take her out and missed the entire thing. And, of course, when we went on honeymoon we left Bonnie behind as well.

That was an event in itself. As I have already said, we did not have much money and so we went off to Cornwall to camp for a week travelling by motorbike. I had the words 'Just married' pinned to my jacket; they did not stay on there long as torrential rain consumed the sign and our journey and most of our time away.

One lasting memory is waking up in our two-man tent and sitting up, with the sides of the tent stuck to either side of my face and the severe condensation running down into my sleeping bag. 'Please, just one night in a B&B,' was my cry. David did oblige but I was missing our daughter and spent a lot of time ringing home checking that she was ok and saying things like, 'Wouldn't Bonnie like it here?'

Our little house provided us with a warm refuge with small cosy rooms; the back boiler in the dining room provided a snug haven for when I would sneak downstairs to feed Bonnie at night when she was little, so as not to disturb David.

I had chosen to live my life outside of God's care in many ways. Still, God never let go of me and I suppose that as David and I celebrate his fiftieth birthday alone together this year we are having a kind of belated honeymoon, and it is brilliant!

During this time I decided I would learn how to run a pre-school. So once a week I attended the local Adult Education Centre. One day someone passed me an advertisement: 'Christian pre-school for sale to a Christian'. I was really excited, but we had no money; I was clothing us from jumble sales – in fact, my best friend and I would peruse the local paper in search of the best ones and we became rather adroit at seeking out the ones whose patrons were well-to-do and so had the best clothes, or furniture, or household appliances. It was a fun time, although the rugby scrum that was often required did depress me sometimes. We would spy the dealers out to get hold of items to sell on and we would be ready as soon as the hall doors opened to dive right in.

So how was I going to raise the funds for the school, let alone get to the place each morning and set it up and run it? Well my family helped out – Dad gave me some money for the deposit, as did David's family, and I agreed to pay the rest in instalments. It was a hectic time, as I was by now pregnant again.

Chapter 12
I can juggle

A new pre-school, and pregnant. I really don't know how I managed it all.

Millie's arrival was amazing. I felt in control; I had done it before, after all. Labour started and I woke, walking around the house while David and Bonnie slept, squatting to ride over the contractions. I was so peaceful. I was married, David and I were happy and Bonnie was wonderful. But could I love another child as much as Bonnie? No problem there: we are made in God's image and He loves us all. So Millie was born, a beautiful baby, a sister for Bonnie, and I was home hours after giving birth; I didn't want Bonnie to feel left out! And Millie had her first school photograph taken at ten days old! My feet, or hers for that matter, did not touch the ground.

I had always been busy, busy, busy. It would not have been unusual for me to be found walking around the supermarket doing the weekly shop with my baby up my leather jacket hidden away snugly breastfeeding; there was always something that I thought I had to do.

So life charged along a mad juggle. I would wake early each morning and sort out the kids, feeding them and trying to sit still to breastfeed Millie, getting all the paraphernalia in the car that you need for babies then dashing across town to set up the equipment. I had transformed the school from a sit-at-your-desk sort of place to a place of free play and learning through play. So each morning I would have to haul out of the shed all the toys: slides, trampolines, bikes, blackboards, sandpit, etc while Millie sat in her buggy and Bonnie amused herself (there were a lot of things she could amuse herself with!), then set up tables, mix paint, get out the puzzles. On and on it went. It required a lot of focused determination, and that remains today. I am a determined woman who wants to do her best but views herself as lazy too. I sound really confused, don't I? On some mornings, to give her an experience with other children, I would drop off Bonnie at our church pre-school or my mum or my sister would take her. It was a juggling act and entailed the help and support of family and friends to succeed.

It was not without its problems. When Bonnie started primary school she only went for the morning. The school was very understanding and allowed her to stay for school lunch so that I could get back for her. But she was the only one in her year who did that and it meant a manic run to get back for her in time. It also meant that I could not take her to school in the morning and had to leave her with David, which was not a good idea because he did not like getting up early (he still doesn't) and she would stand with her faced pressed to the glass front door crying as she watched me drive away. Later on she would go to a neighbour whose daughter was in the same year and go with them. It was very stressful because the underlying reason that I had started the school was that I wanted my children to be with me, and so to cause them upset was terrible for them and me.

The next traumatic event that leaps into my mind was the day when I arrived at the church hall (have I mentioned that my school was run in a church hall?) and bent down to pick up Millie which released the counteracting weight from the front of the buggy and caused the overloaded buggy to fall backwards, dislocating my kneecap on the way! I dropped Millie to the floor where she landed on her padded bottom and I fell to the floor. It was one of those moments where you choose how you react: I had been reading about rejoicing in all circumstances and so I sat there, in pain, trying to think how I was going to rejoice now. I hit the kneecap back into place and struggled up to continue setting up the school, thanking God that I could still walk and that Millie was ok.

I have suffered all my life with hypermobility of my joints; the first time I dislocated my kneecap was when I was lying on my stomach on the front room floor of my friend's parents' house. I moved my leg and my kneecap stayed where it was. I was taken off to hospital with my legs tied together. As I waited in A&E a doctor walked over to the trolley that I was lying on and unceremoniously knocked it back into place. My scream confirmed my thoughts that I would put it back in myself from now on. Over the years it has come out of joint on various occasions; when someone brushed against me with a shopping basket, in bed, any place where there was close contact with people.

This rushed lifestyle continued for nearly ten years, during which time I had a miscarriage. It was such a difficult time. I was devastated. The scan showed that there was no heartbeat. Although I was less than 12 weeks pregnant I was living the life and was thrilled to be pregnant again. God was not absent from me in my grief. I say 'my' grief because I don't think David was as affected as I was. It was my body that had to have a D&C, my hormones that cried out, my empty womb that ached. I still recall a lovely friend giving me a Twila Paris song – 'The warrior's a child' – that gave me permission to cry and weep.

Once again God used Psalm 139 to speak to me to bind up my hurts.

You have searched me, Lord, and you know me.
You know when I sit and when I rise;
you perceive my thoughts from afar.
You discern my going out and my lying down;
you are familiar with all my ways.
Before a word is on my tongue
you, Lord, know it completely.

You hem me in behind and before,
and you lay your hand upon me.
Such knowledge is too wonderful for me,
too lofty for me to attain.

Where can I go from your Spirit?
Where can I flee from your presence?
If I go up to the heavens, you are there;
if I make my bed in the depths, you are there.
If I rise on the wings of the dawn,
if I settle on the far side of the sea,
even there your hand will guide me,
your right hand will hold me fast.
If I say, 'Surely, the darkness will hide me
and the light become night around me,'
even the darkness will not be dark to you;
the night will shine like the day,
for darkness is as light to you.

For you created my inmost being;
you knit me together in my mother's womb.
I praise you because I am fearfully and wonderfully
made;
your works are wonderful,
I know that full well.
My frame was not hidden from you
when I was made in the secret place,
when I was woven together in the depths of the earth.
Your eyes saw my unformed body;
all the days ordained for me were written in your book
before one of them came to be.

How precious to me are your thoughts, God!
How vast is the sum of them!
Were I to count them,

they would outnumber the grains of sand –
when I awake, I am still with you.

If only you, God, would slay the wicked!
Away from me, you who are bloodthirsty!
They speak of you with evil intent;
your adversaries misuse your name.
Do I not hate those who hate you, Lord,
and abhor those who are in rebellion against you?
I have nothing but hatred for them;
I count them my enemies.
Search me, God, and know my heart;
test me and know my anxious thoughts.
See if there is any offensive way in me,
and lead me in the way everlasting.

In fact, He gave me a picture in my mind of the child I lost;
he was a boy. I can still see his face. I believe I will see him
whole in heaven one day.

Chapter 13
Puppy mayhem

We were told to wait a while before trying to have another baby, but you know me, I am impatient – Hollie arrived three years after Millie.

She was a delightful child who, being the youngest, did not bother to talk; she would just point and scream and we all knew what she wanted. At around two years old she started to talk and has not stopped. It was Hollie that I was pregnant with when I thought God told me that David would have a son. My first words to her were, 'I'm so sorry, I have been talking to you as if you were a boy!'

The next arrival in our family was brown and black with a tail. I know I am crazy! Sometimes I get a bee in my bonnet and there is no stopping me. Between Christmas and New Year when Hollie was 18 months old I decided that I needed to get a puppy to complete our little family. We had extended our kitchen and I suppose I needed to fill the space!

We were checked by the RSPCA and told we could have a dog. A dog! I wanted a puppy, not a dog that could potentially savage my children. No, I could only have a dog because my little girl might hurt a puppy!

I was not impressed and was steam rolling ahead on my mission to find one somewhere else when I remembered that one of the children from my school had told me that she had a new puppy. So on New Year's Eve I rang her mother who informed me that she thought that there was one left. I dragged everyone round there to see it: there was the mum – a long-haired German shepherd – and the dad – a cross Rottweiler!

I can almost hear you gasping, but I am afraid it was love at first sight. Cleo, as we named her, had to be ours.

Life was now even more hectic. I'm not sure how I managed, like who looked after Cleo when I was working, but I do remember how we discovered the common and the woods. This is what happened the first time I let her off the lead. I had taken her to puppy training so I should have known better. She was about four months old and an adorable little thing that would follow me around; in fact, when we went to see her the first time the owners had nicknamed her 'Always' because she always was there by your side. So there I was with my now two-year-old daughter in her buggy and the puppy trotting alongside when the bells in the adjacent church started to toll. And that innocent ball of fluff started to run. My, 'Stop, Cleo!' was shouted to deaf ears. I started to run after her, pushing my buggy and manically screaming. A group of older ladies watched the scenario unfolding before their eyes.

'Please can you look after my baby?' I said as I thrust my sleeping daughter's buggy into their hands. Out across the car park Cleo ran, turning right as she started down the road that cut across the common. A man in a car pulled up next to me.

'Hop in love, we'll catch it.'

Cleo legged it down the hill and around the pond with us in hot pursuit. Eventually she ran into a garden and I managed to corner her under a bush. Soaked in urine (the puppy, not me), I clasped the terrified little thing to my chest and my knight in shining armour drove us back to the woods. Meanwhile, the group of ladies waited patiently for the strange woman to reappear. I had actually left my child with strangers to chase after a dog!

It's interesting how things work out. Only a year or so ago I met one of the ladies who had comforted me on my return with Cleo: she was walking into the building where I work. She is a counsellor too.

So a puppy (a slightly manic, furniture- and doorframe-eating one), and now a third daughter – making three – and running a pre-school. I am surprised that I don't need more hair dye than I already use. Life was pretty crazy.

I was the mother of three fantastic little girls, my husband had become a Christian and we were happy. I had been running a lovely pre-school that was highly esteemed and I was walking closely with God. Life was good.

Chapter 14
I will repay the years

Out of the blue an article appeared in a free local newspaper. It read, 'Children in need of love' and the article that followed described children who were in need of a home for various reasons. They were children whose parents were alcoholics and drug addicts and who had been affected by their addictions. I immediately thought, maybe I can pay something back, I could explain to these children that their mother had been ill; I had insider knowledge after all.

I spoke to David about it. We were at this time about to go to a Christian holiday camp called Spring Harvest. Butlins campuses are taken over by Spring Harvest once a year and families spend a holiday there receiving teaching from amazing speakers, the children have their own entertainment, there is great worship in the Big Top and a good time is had by all. So we decided that we would both pray separately about it and see what happened.

So we did. I sought God and had this experience: I went into the Big Top (which is the main venue for teaching at the event) in the evening after a session where people were actively seeking God's Holy Spirit, and there were a few people standing around near the stage. I sat in the back and asked God what I should do, and He gave me this vision (God often speaks to me through pictures in my mind; some come from the Bible, and some not): I saw the train of His robe flowing down. This referred, I believed, to Isaiah 6:1. As I leant down into it, it moved; well, it kind of billowed. My words as I have recalled this story many times were that it was like solid air. Fluid yet holding, and I heard God tell me that adopting a child would not hurt my family. He, of course, knew that having that information was the most important piece of knowledge He could give me because I was passionate about my children, like most mothers, and had gone out of my way to ensure that I cared for them myself in their early years as much as possible. It was also a word for David because he is intrinsically practical and concerned about me overstretching (nothing new there then!). I was thrilled to hear from God.

So with that picture I called the number in the newspaper. The lovely lady told me, to my disappointment, that they had had a massive response. I asked about the criteria for adoption and she said that the child I adopted would have to be two years younger than my youngest child. As I had a two-year-old and was a 40-year-old mother of three, I thought that they were not going to give me a baby. The lady assured me, however, that they were not looking at my needs but at the needs of the child. At this point I need to tell you that all the children in the newspaper were over two years old, so I thought our chances were slim. As we drove home we discussed the situation, and David told me that God had not told him anything but that he had a sense of peace every time he prayed. Well that was that for me – as far as I was concerned it was a green light!

Social services eventually rang me and told me the date of a meeting about the children. To my disappointment and irritation (to put it mildly), David was unable to come, so I went alone. I think I was the only person there without a partner.

As I entered the room I saw pieces of A4 paper stuck on the wall. As I started to read one of these profiles, I thought, 'Oh, you're David's son', and I had a sudden realisation that there in the room was information on David's future son! I had heard God after all, which I suppose is a lesson on the perfection of His timing. It is His timing, not ours.

So we started the nine-month process that eventually led to our son's arrival. We had to attend courses that we found very difficult. Discussing private issues (our sexual practices, for example) and being the only ones on the training who already had kids. That was an eye opener: hearing people's expectations of parenthood and observing how the facilitators corrected their views! We had to drive quite a distance to these meetings and knew each time that they would be uncomfortable. So on it went.

During the summer of the same year I went off to India to sing backing vocals with my sister in my uncle's band. We did a two-and-a-half-week tour of universities in various cities all around India. And that is another story: it was out of God's grace that I was given the opportunity to experience that most wonderful land and not be off my face on drugs this time. It was one of the many ways that God told me that I could not pay back the price of freedom and salvation.

While I was in India God gave me a verse for our future son; it comes from the book of Joel: 'I will repay you for the years the locusts have eaten' (Joel 2:25).

It was a verse for him, so we gave our son Lewis the middle name of Joel, and the words were for me. For God in His wisdom has given me the greatest honour, the honour of giving me a son who did not come from my body, and is trusting me to raise him with God's help.

The years that I had spent as an addict were not going to limit God's generosity. I often stand absolutely astonished that He would bless me that much. It's a bit like leading worship in church: I think that God has a great sense of humour – an ex-addict leading! But on the other hand I know, I mean, I *really* know, how much He loves me and how much I am a forgiven woman. Maybe that is what equips us to be worship leaders – we need to worship passionately.

While I was in India, David was holding the fort and being interviewed by Social Services – the S.S. as he called them!

Poor him, he was not impressed. On my return it was my go, and eventually we were shown a picture of the child that they wanted to match us with. David rushed off to get a copy of it! 'Do you think you could love this little boy?' they asked. Of course we could!

After that it was a roller coaster ride. Our social worker did a lot of work with our children in preparation. I hassled to meet him and eventually got my way. It was so amazing; I loved him at first sight. My lovely husband was working but managed to get to the house before me, so I have a wonderful video of me arriving at the house walking in the door and us both seeing each other (my son and I) for the first time: it is very special.

Now remember that I wanted to adopt a child of a drug addict in order to pay something back? Well, God had other ideas: our son has no history of drug or alcohol abuse in his family; in fact, when the newspaper article that I had read had gone to print, he had only just been born.

Lewis officially became our son a month before his first birthday, can you believe it? A 40-year-old woman adopting a wonderful baby boy – how God has blessed me! Now I don't say that in any way to show off; it's just that it is so undeserved and His love is so undeserved, don't you think? If you are reading this and thinking that He doesn't love you, remember: you can't earn it, He does love you, and He chose and chooses the most unlikely people to bless.

Do you remember that I gave my grandmother's ring to a dealer and never got it back? Well on my fortieth birthday my mother gave me a ring box. When I opened it I discovered a pearl ring; it was exactly the same as the one I had given away. My parents had no idea about what I had done. I would never have told them as I was too ashamed. But God knew, and in that moment I experienced Him telling me that He loved me and that the ring was a symbol of the restorative love of God. My mother could not believe it when I told her. I suppose for her it meant that a thought had turned into a moment for God to speak. He is so kind.

Chapter 15
James One

It was around this time, when I had had my pre-school for nearly ten years, that I started to think that God was pointing me towards training as a counsellor. I had been spending more time with mums in the kitchen listening to their troubles and it appeared to be the next step. Lo and behold, a leaflet came through my door about the counselling course at the local college. I have always been impulsive (just in case you have forgotten), so I automatically assumed that this was God's guidance, which, it turned out, was right.

I started to do the first courses in the evenings. The question was, would I see it through and do the Advanced Diploma?

Lewis had arrived and the rules for pre-schools had changed and I was not allowed to take my new son into school. So a lovely lady called Rosemary took over the running of the school. She was brilliant, very organised and professional, but I think that when the main person, in this case me, is not around, things change. The school was my baby and I was very enthusiastic, as was Rosemary, but even so, numbers started to drop.

I was in church one day when they mentioned that the toddler group that was running one morning a week needed help. I felt challenged about it; I can clearly recall going downstairs on the day it ran and peering through the doors and saying to God, 'I can't do this; those women look far too scary, and anyway I run a pre-school not a toddler group!' How arrogant I was!

My pastor at the time was a very challenging man, and it would be fair to say we had a love–hate relationship. But one thing I remember that he said challenged me: 'You have a butterfly nature, always flitting around from one thing to the other.' I was not offended; I heard him. I believe it was that that pushed me to get involved in the toddler group.

I got off my self-imposed high horse and I quickly got the group organised (I was used to running a pre-school after all!). I extended the days to two mornings a week. I loved it; I loved the women and the children. It was rather stressful, though, as my son had become a child who bit other children: I can still see in my mind's eye the huge teeth marks that he left on a little girl's cheek!

It was at this time that, for reasons I did not understand, I was prevented from leading worship by the same pastor. It was awful; I felt bereft and also very insecure. I just had to be obedient, which was a rather tall order for someone like me who did not like authority figures. I knew that God had put me under authority in the church. I cannot really believe I can even type that sentence considering what I used to think. It was a steep learning curve, but God is faithful and His timing was perfect once again, and when I eventually started to lead again I was ready; I was no longer a pre-school leader and had moved on in my counselling.

Around this time I had a picture from God: I was behind with my Bible readings so when we were away on holiday (another gift from God via Eric and Jenny who let us stay every summer for years in their bungalow by the sea), I went up on the roof to read and pray, just like Peter did in the book of Acts. I was reading the book of James and God made me focus on the last verses of the first chapter:

Religion that God our Father accepts as pure and faultless is this: to look after orphans and widows in their distress and to keep oneself from being polluted by the world.

As I continued to sit there with God, He gave me a vision. I asked God for a name for the vision: 'James One'. So I typed it out; this is what the original copy said:

James One.
I went up onto the rooftop patio to seek God and to find out what He wanted me to do next. I knew that He wanted me to close my school and that a new season in my life was beginning. The question was, what did God require of me?
I started to pray and read my daily reading which was the book of James; suddenly I knew that God was talking to me.
'Religion that God the Father accepts as pure and faultless is this; to look after widows and orphans and to keep oneself from being polluted by the world.'
This is what I heard: set up a house, could be a terraced house – just an ordinary house in an ordinary street. There will be a room for play therapy, a room for counselling, a room for parenting courses and for general advice and support.
This could possibly be the start of something big – set up a charitable organisation that is prepared to stand in the gap that family break-up has created.
The aim.
To help mainly women and children get to grips with their situations, to assist if necessary with parenting skills, to love and support.
To help women and children come to terms with their grief.
To provide support that family break-up has destroyed.

To enlighten, empower and enrich through Christian love.

A sanctuary, a way forward.

2nd September 1999

I was unsure what to do with this vision so I gave copies to the elders of my church. Then one day I was talking to one of them and he said there was someone he wanted me to meet. It turned out to be a lady I had met before, when I had attended a parenting course that she was running in my church. There she stood on my front door step and we knew each other instantly. God's hand was apparent again. She worked for a Christian charity.

Not long after, I was taken on as the first counselling placement at Fegans Child and Family Care. The charity was set up in the Victorian days by Mr James Fegan to look after street boys. The amazing thing about it is that the head office of the organisation is run from an ordinary terraced house in an ordinary street. They were counselling people there and they were in the process of equipping a new play therapy room! I could not believe it: it was the house God was talking about.

***

So I decided to close my school and I was able to give a lot of my school equipment to help set up the first play therapy room. The rest of the equipment went to the now newly named 'Bikes and Slides' – the revamped toddler group that was thriving with new mums and kids. The once scary mums were now excited to hear what I was doing and were supportive as I started to train in earnest.

Like most things in life, we need the support of others to achieve our goals. I was no exception. One friend, Anna, looked after Lewis, taking him to playschool while I did my training at college and counselled in a local school and office. My dad agreed to support me by coming round every Monday after school to look after the children and feed them baked beans on toast (it's a well-balanced meal, don't you know?). I suppose I should explain that my relationship with my dad oscillated between him loving me and believing in me and him being angry with me, or me being angry with him. He fed the kids for almost two years, quite a feat really, and then for some strange reason, which caused another fallout, he stopped. So I trained and trained and tried to be the mum and wife I was meant to be.

Chapter 16
Ministry of reconciliation

A few years ago I was leading worship in our church. I had weathered the storm of the previous pastor who had stopped me leading worship and I was now back doing what I loved.

In many ways it was a miracle that I was able to stand at the front of this mostly white middle-class church and feel so free to finally be myself. During the service I had spoken about how important it was to not leave Jesus at home when we go on holiday. At the end of the service a man came and spoke to me; he told me that he believed that God had an important message to give me on my summer holiday.

That year we had found a house to rent in France, so off we set with our four children and two nans squeezed into our, new to us, people carrier. Just outside Chichester on the outward journey the engine blew up in the outside lane of a dual carriage way as we approached a roundabout. We had only had the car a matter of months! Smoke started to fill the car.

Suddenly a man came and helped David push the car to the side of the road. My daughter remembers him as having a strange blond haircut and wearing sunglasses, and I remember saying to David that I thought he was an angel; he was not convinced. But I tell you, he came from nowhere and disappeared afterwards. So there we were, stranded on the side of a very busy roundabout. We were not impressed, but determined to get to our destination. Several calls to the ferry enabled us to get a later booking. Many, many calls enabled us to finally track down an eight-seater car that David's mother rented for us. I just kept thinking God had something that He wanted to tell me; I had to get there.

So eventually we arrived at our destination.

The next morning a family moved in next door – a Pentecostal lady preacher, called Pauline, and her family. I jumped to conclusions as usual and asked to speak to her. I told her all about what had happened and mentioned that maybe she would be able to tell me what God was saying. I was not prepared for her question: 'Do you have the gift of tongues?' I admitted that I did and confessed that I did not use it enough. She told me that I should start to speak them out and seek God and that when He had told me what He wanted from me I should go back and see her and then she would pray for me.

Tongues, the speaking of a heavenly language, was something I had asked God for years before. My journey to receive them started at Spring Harvest long before my husband became a Christian. I had gone with my friend Cheryl and one evening I had taken myself off to a seminar on the Holy Spirit. I was rather nervous anyway when suddenly at the front of the meeting people started to wail and shout and fall down. I was out of that place like a shot, marching across the campus railing at God, 'I have had enough extreme stuff in my life. I don't want any more!'

Clutching my Diet Coke (it's funny the details we remember), I strode back to our chalet. The next morning, or maybe even that night, I was singing in the bath and Cheryl was banging on the door asking me if I had been drinking. God gave me one word that night in tongues and so I used it as I praised Him. (Tongues are written about in the Bible in Acts 2:4 when the disciples were filled with the Holy Spirit and started to speak in different languages.)

Now remember I am a somewhat demanding woman. I wanted a language like the ones I had read about in the Bible where a tongue was spoken and it turned out to be a real language. I wanted a language I could use to praise God because I believed that I was not eloquent enough. Gradually, over the course of a few years, God gave me another word. But I was worried and so sought a good friend to pray with me. I was worried that I was forcing it. It was in her home that I saw a vision of Jesus. He walked towards me and put His hand under my chin and looked into my eyes and told me wordlessly that if I kept my eyes focused on Him it would be alright. Can you imagine me hurtling home, rushing upstairs and finally relinquishing my tongue into His hands? It was truly brilliant.

Years later at a 'Jews for Jesus' talk at our church, I approached a lady to ask her about my language. One word God had given me was 'Adonai', a Hebrew word. As I started to speak out the other words she told me that they were Hebrew too. God hears our prayers, and sometimes says yes!

So back to France! How ridiculous to hassle God for the gift and then not use it. I am almost blushing with embarrassment as I write because I hardly ever use it even now.

A week of praying finally resulted in God telling me that He wanted to use me for a ministry of reconciliation. I was to talk with people one-to-one, in small groups, in larger groups and, here I hesitate to tell you, that I would talk to them in large auditoriums. The last bit still sounds wild, crazy, but I must believe God for it. He also said that I would be used to reconcile people to God and to each other. I was really shocked and also excited. So off I trotted to see Pauline the Pentecostal minister and to tell her. She listened to me and said that was a big gift and we needed to go out for a walk because she would like her son-in-law to pray for me too, but that he made a lot of noise when he prayed. Oh my life, what was I letting myself in for?

So off we went in the middle of rural Brittany, down a lane in the middle of the night with only the moon for light. They started to pray for me and I found myself on the ground laughing; I could not stop. God had floored me.

Suddenly the son-in-law said to me, 'Tell me about your father.'

'Why?' was my shocked reply.

'Because whenever I have prayed for you this week, God has told me that he is your stumbling block.'

I could not believe it; this man knew nothing about me and God was speaking the truth through him.

So they prayed for me, and I have slowly, bit by bit, tried to forgive my dad. Forgiveness seems to be a hard-fought thing to attain. But I have finally made it now. I still get mad with him but I do forgive him.

So the ministry of reconciliation: I thought it was about worship, and in a way it is. But more than that, I believe it is about my work in counselling and supporting individuals and families to live a better life. Sometimes it is about helping them to regain their faith and sometimes it is about enabling them to live with their broken, imperfect bodies and minds.

Chapter 17
Menopausal swing

Nine years on I had what is known as a Birmingham resurfacing – a partial hip replacement. It was horrible. I have very clear memories of my lovely friend Sarah coming down to see me and washing me; her care overwhelmed me. It's strange the situations God puts us in to experience love and care. It was very humbling.

Six weeks later, on my first day back at work, I let my client out of the back gate, turned to walk down my garden path and found myself unable to move. Fortunately my daughter was home, where I work as a therapist. I yelled that I couldn't move my leg. It had felt a bit odd when I had been walking on the common that morning, but I was really unable to move my leg now. Somehow Bonnie got me into the house and called David, who was working not too far away. He came home and called my consultant who told him that I had to get to hospital. Bonnie immediately phoned some Christian friends who set up a prayer chain (a group of people who prayed that I would be ok). So I arrived in my local A&E department while people were talking to God for me.

'We need to x-ray it to make sure it's ok, but I am 99% sure it is ok.'

The young doctor was sure I was ok as I had no pain and could move myself around on the bed, but I could not walk. He stuck his head around the curtain once he had the results and said, 'You know, don't you? It's fractured.'

'He will divorce me,' I shouted, my voice echoing around the ward.

My husband looked aghast!

I had a very difficult recovery the first time round and I thought David would not put up with me having another operation. And the idea that they would have to open up the scar again was too much to bear; I had only had it done seven weeks before. It was madness. Still, there was no alternative.

This time my healing process was relatively pain free; it was just strange doing it all again. All my plans to get back to work had been put on hold, all my clients had to wait again and seven weeks became 14. My family had, once again, to put up with their mum being incapacitated. It was no joke.

But we all survived and life has continued, and the children have grown up a bit. I am now an experienced therapist seeing a wide variety of clients in private practice. But life was not all smooth running; the menopause had arrived with all its many twists and turns, including weight gain and hormonal swings. Take the following:

One day as I lay in bed, unable to sleep, David arrived. Banging against the bed, he dropped his key-laden trousers on the floor and turned on the fluorescent screen of a hand-held computer that is more his companion than I am these days. I have often been resentful of the attention he pays to his screens.

'Turn it off,' I muttered in a grumpy tone that I suddenly heard with clarity.

'Don't be grumpy.'

'Sorry.'

I had heard myself and I really did not want to be a grumpy old woman any more, but I appeared to be one.

Then I started to mumble, revealing my vulnerability – you know the usual stuff, 'I don't feel attractive, don't you fancy me any more?' There followed comments about common interests and the lack of them, and I made mention of the fact that he had tugged down my rising t-shirt at lunchtime.

His tender response was, 'Well it was unattractive.'

'But no one was here.'

'But it's not nice. How would you like it if I walked around with my spare tyre out?'

That was it for me!

Now I sit alone in the kitchen with hot milk by my side that is aimed to settle me. The desire to write has overcome me.

Shall I call this book *From hourglass to pot-bellied*?

I don't know; but I know that today, 29th March 2009, is the day that I started to try and get it all under control.

I am NOT going to sink into depression, I am NOT going to be reliant on my lovely (and I do mean that) husband suddenly developing the gift of flattery, I have to face facts. I HAVE BECOME AN OVERWEIGHT, MIDDLE-AGED WOMAN. The question is, how can I do this thing called weight loss? At this moment the plan is to keep a detailed diary of the journey. The thought of buying secret bathroom scales moves rapidly across my mind, a smile flickers around the corners of my mouth as I take stock of the situation. This is not going to be a quick-fix thing; my red dressing gown does me no favours, and I start to see what my husband sees as well.

Cellulite! It's everywhere, like some invading army has taken over my skin, from legs to arms and tummy. In fact, it must have been on my tummy before because I remember years ago David calling me the Pillsbury Dough girl – an advertising campaign from years ago, so feel free to use the internet to look it up! Now I have expanded and the body that used to grace the pages of magazines has an extra eight inches on all areas.

How did it happen?

Well, I suppose it happened the way it always does, when other things become more important. Children, for instance, and work and marriage. It's funny, I look at my daughter and see the weight just fall off her and I recognise that for her food is not that important, the way it used to be not important to me. She has other things on her mind and does not need food

105

to take up the slack the way it has for me. So how do I deal with it? A change of focus might help.

Now that in itself is strange because it means that I have actually got to focus on food in order not to focus on it so much; that sounds absolutely bonkers, but I have to give it a go.

We have a Father in heaven who loves us and longs to spend time with us. He is interested in our lives and wants us to talk about those things with Him; He waits with eager anticipation for us to reveal the passions and desires of our hearts. He loves people, loves their little ways and, like a lot of parents, loves to see parts of Him reflected in His kids. He is, as I read one day in a Bible study, sitting in a room in our lives, a fire is blazing, a seat is pulled up next to Him ready for us to come and sit on, and we keep walking past the open door.

Why do we do that?

To answer that question I'm going to write a weekly journal of what it means to be a daughter of the King. Now that in itself is no mean feat because, as you will find out, I keep walking past the room with the chair in it.

Chapter 18
Chicks are flying

It is 1:45 am and night finally does that special thing that only it can do – it removes all air from the room and forces me to finally leap out of bed to let in more night from outside, a night full of oxygen that enables me to face reality. I cannot sleep. Tomorrow Millie goes to university. Tomorrow everything changes.

Fresh oxygen brings to the forefront of my mind the thoughts I thought I had dealt with in the previous weeks, thoughts that all mothers are veterans at. Thoughts and prayers, protection prayers, as she awakes that first morning or even as she goes to sleep that first night, prayers that she will make safe decisions and that men and women who are evil will keep away.

I gasp in the oxygen that the night wind blows towards my pillow but it is not enough, and tears, hot and burning, persist even through my fingers, pressed urgently against my surprised eyes.

Loving each of my children has never been difficult; the amazing muscle that is the human heart just expands and embraces fully each child. With that knowledge ringing in through my tinnitus that is louder at night, I realise I am tired and maybe sleep will come now. Tears must wait or I will wake with eyes like a boxer, like I used to have when I was young after a fight with my dad.

'I have to leave her with you, Lord,' I mumble in my mind.

'It's ok,' is the faint response.

In the darkness that is oppressing but not suppressing my tears I fumble for something to write with. A random thought had entered my awareness: *Before Millie*. Call the book *Before Millie*.

I have not thought of my book for a while now, I had put it, metaphorically speaking, on the back burner. But there it is as plain as day. David stirs and puts out his hand. 'Is it Millie?' I can only nod in the blackness.

Eventually I get up and mumble something about getting a drink and coming back in a bit. As I move towards the door with thoughts of hot milk, I reach out for my dressing gown and suddenly realise I have been here before. Bonnie, our eldest daughter, had gone to Uganda and the same thing had happened, and the solution had been the same – hot milk and writing. There is a comfort in knowing that love is painful but survivable.

The thing is, did I treasure each moment, and was I a good enough mother? The answer to the latter question is probably yes, but treasuring each moment? Many for sure, but life is full and responsibilities are many... too many moments were not tasted fully and enjoyed in all their loveliness. But as I sit here – it is now 2:40 am – memories flood in thick and fast, too many to share and, to be quite honest, would you be interested in them? The little girl who from a very early age knew her own mind is leaving tomorrow, and I am praying that the young woman who will walk the campus will also follow her heart and her Lord as she desires today.

I am going to miss her, and as my fingers touch the 'm' of 'miss' the tears come unbidden and I am struggling to see the screen. I want her to go to be free to engage in all that God has in store for her; miss her I will, but tomorrow I must smile and hug and save my tears for the journey home, I hope.

'So how did you manage the difficult things before?' I recognise the whisper of the Creator. 'You have come so far; how did you do it?'

'I am not sure, Lord,' I hear myself whisper. 'I am not sure that I have come that far really. I suppose I am in a different place to where I started but, far? It really is not that far, is it?'

The following day, weary to my bones, I stick on my smile. The car is packed to the gunnels and David and I transport our precious daughter and all her belongings to Reading and, you know what, I did manage it. We did get her settled, we did eat lunch out and then, after we said our goodbyes to our very excited second-born and were driving away, I bawled my eyes out.

Chapter 19
Journaling begins

So let's start this journal. After a full-on week of long-awaited appointments, I enter the weekend where I am going to stay with a close relative for curry, wine and chat, with a raging headache. As I drive across Kent, to my great delight travelling in the opposite direction to all the traffic, I recognise that old familiar feeling. The feeling of, hang on, I don't think I have seen much of my Father God recently.

Are you like that? Do you run headlong and then get brought up short, out of breath and then realise that you are running metaphorically on the wrong fuel? Diesel instead of unleaded and you suddenly find yourself stuck in a lay-by or, worse still, in the middle of the motorway in grave danger of being mown down.

When I run on the wrong fuel you can be pretty sure that I will be involved in a car crash of relationships, and that weekend was no exception. After a great sleepover full of laughter and chat I drove home. Still in the back of my mind I was aware that I had not checked in with God.

The next morning, still no call to God, and it happens.

Rage, yes that old chestnut, reared its head. It bypassed sadness and hurt and started to drive me at 100 mph towards anyone in my path. The trouble with rage is that, although it is a dangerous emotion, it also gets things done. It energises me.

So I get what I want sorted and then try to be still. Impossible; I am still running on the spot, my engine is on a fast tickover and very close to boiling point.

I went to the evening service out of a sense of duty, to support my children. Thank goodness I had not lost that in my rage. Once there I was still irritated by the things we were being asked to do. It was a very interactive service and, as someone who leads it once a month, I was now experiencing increased empathy for those who come to those services but who find it hard to participate. But God had other ideas and eventually broke through in His usual way where I am concerned, through a song and I started to listen out for His still small voice.

I left the hall where we were meeting in order to spend some time alone with God. (This often happens as part of our services, but this time I was the only one who went. It is often too hard for people to move out of their comfort zones and out of their seats.) Anyway there I was in a youth meeting room with my son, whom I discovered bouncing up and down on a Pilates ball.

'I have come to pray,' I muttered. 'So you need to be quiet.'

As my 12-year-old son sat on the huge silver ball, I prayed and asked God for a Bible verse.

'Please, God, give me a verse.' Then the words 'Hebrews 12' came into my mind. But I was suddenly terrified. What if there is no chapter? What if Hebrews ends at chapter 10? Then that would mean you don't exist. Oh my goodness, I really am having a crisis. Carefully I turned the pages and there it was:

Therefore, since we are surrounded by such a great crowd of witnesses, let us throw off everything that hinders and the sin that so easily entangles. And let us run with perseverance the race marked out for us, fixing our eyes on Jesus...
Hebrews 12:1-2

Well there you go! You ask God to speak and He does. I could see it all so clearly. I was full of rage because I was not spending time with God. I was advising other people to do it and I was not doing it enough myself. I realised that in order to shake off sin we need to use a great deal of energy. It is not a casual shaking off; it is an active, energised action that is focused on the task in hand.

I was being disciplined by my Father in heaven, but I love it when He does that because for some strange reason I don't feel condemned by Him. I actually feel joy that He is talking to me. So I left church with a determination to be obedient.

The following morning found me alone with God. I sat in my little room looking out on my garden pondering my stupidity; the drive, the momentum that can mean that I ride roughshod over those I love, and I saw hanging in my garden a glass jar designed to catch wasps. I have to confess that I didn't know what it was for until one day I saw wasps etched on the glass. Anyway, you put sweet water in it, you carefully pour the water in the top and it runs down the side and rests in the up-turned lip that surrounds the hole at the bottom where the wasps enter. They enter to gorge themselves on the sweetness and then discover that they cannot find their way out.

Sin is the same; it lures us with the sweet aroma, calls us to enjoy, it's there after all, and then we enter and are caught in a trap of our own making.

The glass jar in my garden was different; the cork stopper that used to be in the top had dissolved away over the years.

Sin, for me, and for you for that matter, used to be a trap, but Jesus has removed the stopper. I can still enter, and sometimes I do, but the stopper is removed, so I just need to fly out the top, like the wasps can do from mine.

God has often sent blue tits to confirm His presence to me. It started many years ago when I was preparing a service in my room and I was struggling to think. I had finally been given inspiration by God and was just leaving my room and blue tits appeared; I heard a kind of plopping noise and looked down. There on the ground sat a perfect blue tit, so I bent down and picked it up. It just sat on my hand looking at me. Then I heard another sound and looked down, and there were two more. I couldn't believe it. I picked them up as well.

So there I was holding three perfect, beautiful birds, blue and yellow and so calm. I had no idea what to do, so I did what any self-respecting person would do: I took a picture on my phone. Then, as they sat on my hand, one cupped in my palm and the others using my index finger for a perch, I walked into my kitchen and rang the local animal rescue place. They advised me to put them in a box, as I had a cat, and bring them in. It was a rather strange scene, me walking about emptying out cereal boxes trying to find a container.

In the end I had another plan. I went outside, raised my hand to the sky and stood there. One by one the birds opened their wings and flew off. It was one of the loveliest moments in my life and God confirmed that He was, indeed, in the house.

Ever since that day He has revealed His presence in that way, flocks of blue tits following me as I walk and pray on the common or a tree full of them as I am praying for someone.

So after spending time with God that week and Him talking about sin entangling me, it was no surprise when I became aware of a blue tit flying around. 'Come back!' my spirit cried. Suddenly it was there, a foot from my face, sitting on the fence looking at me, confirmation that God was guiding me.

Chapter 20
Alcohol diminishes His voice

This week my husband and I did our usual sortie to Northern Ireland to stay with friends. It is an annual event. The men watch the bike racing and us girls talk and maybe shop, go out for coffee and then talk some more.

Now my friend Kim has been in my life for about ten years and has been very instrumental in God speaking to me about my use of alcohol. Now just to get the picture straight, I am not an alcoholic, but I have been a drug addict so I have issues around substances with addictive potential.

Over the past ten years Kim has often been there when God has challenged me on my drinking, and considering that she does not live near me, that is no mean feat. I can tell you, we all need a Kim in life, someone who understands our weaknesses because they are reflected in her, so she can do that straight talking thing that I both love and hate.

This week, before my arrival in Ireland, has been full of events: Monday – a fun birthday meal with a very good friend which included alcohol. Tuesday – time spent supporting friends with problems in their marriage which included us drinking a bottle of wine. Wednesday found me arguing with my son and then drinking two gin and tonics alone in my bedroom! The next day we are on the plane going to Ireland when I find myself wanting a Jack Daniels and Coke – I am on holiday after all! So there I sit between David and a man I have never met before. We strike up a conversation about, of all things, Jack blooming Daniels and he recalls times when he has drunk it. God is now starting to speak in my mind, and then the man says that he will be in a bar near to where we are staying on the Sunday, and I do *not* say that I will be in church.

Now that may not sound like a big deal, but to those who know me, to not mention God *is* a big deal for me.

We arrived at our friends' home and Kim gets down to it.

'How is the drink going? We still have the rum you brought last year.'

Quick as anything I respond with, 'I am still drinking, but I *have* written a book.'

Now even I can tell that I am being defensive. We both laugh and I tell her what has happened this week.

'You know that you have to lay it on the altar,' she says.

'Oh no, not again,' I think.

***

It had happened before, in my forty-ninth year. I had gone to a friend's bonfire night party and had consumed the punch without noticing how much I had drunk. Then a friend who respects me came up to talk to me, and I could see written all over her face her dismay that I had drunk too much. It was awful, and too late – I could not make myself sober in that moment.

The next morning found me in a repentant mood in church, and God spoke straight into my heart and told me to lay it down. I turned around almost expecting Kim to be there, and there she was; I could not believe it. She smiled at me and I knew that she had heard it too. I did stop drinking – no mean feat on the run-up to Christmas. It was a big deal, and I let everyone know.

So now I am back in Ireland and the same conversation is happening all over again.

'You can't put on new clothes until you have taken off the old ones,' she says.

I love the way people speak in different ways, don't you? In Ireland they say 'take a drink'.

Kim says, 'I don't take a drink in company,' by which she means when she is out of her home. The wisdom was coming thick and fast: the Bible says keep away from even the appearance of evil. Psalm 119:115 says, 'Away from me, you evildoers, that I may keep the commands of my God!'

So that was that. There and then I decide to stop, and I empty the rum down the sink.

That night finds me sitting in my bed reading my Bible reading notes, and Jeff Lucas does it again.

'The bottle is not the answer' is written in large letters across the page: I laugh out loud. God is so specific sometimes, isn't he?

It is different this time. I am embracing life without drink rather than not drinking. It is easier too. I don't feel the need to tell everyone (although I am telling you!). I am just living my life.

***

Above all else, guard your heart, for everything you do flows from it.
Proverbs 4:23

This is my aim: to allow God to have more of my heart, but how can I relinquish more of my own desire? It seems like an impossible task. And I fail at almost every turn.

Like many people, I am a rescuer by instinct. Well, we are made in God's image, and He is a rescuer, isn't he? The difference is that my rescuer often appears to operate out of my control and I am not even aware that I am in rescuer mode. The other day I became so angry when I tried to protect someone I love from being hurt. It rose up in me like lava and

I just acted. Now that is not what God does, so my family likeness to Him needs a vast amount of refining.

Why are we so reactive? I mean, He, God, feels our pain and He is not like us, so why can't I do it? What can I do to stop my reactive nature and yet retain my passion for justice?

I need to hold back: I have just had foot surgery which means I cannot put my foot down for at least two weeks and will then have to wear a plaster for six weeks, so it looks like the ideal opportunity to try to practise holding myself in check.

Just so you know, I am not a particularly tidy person, but there are certain things that I like done and, of course, I now have to ask for practically every one of them to be done. I am only five days in!

But I have read a novel already and now I am aiming to finish the three books that I am in the middle of as well!

In *The Weight of Glory* by C.S Lewis is found the following gem:

We are half hearted creatures fooling about with drink and sex and ambition (and religious effort) when infinite joy is offered us, like an ignorant child who wants to go on making mud pies in a slum because he cannot imagine what is meant by the offer of a holiday at the sea. We are far too easily pleased.

I want that. But how, I am so fickle?

I feel good when I am asked to do an important job. I feel good when I am praised. I feel good when I lose weight. I feel good when my husband compliments me (of course, I have fallen over in shock as well!).

So the journey continues.

Chapter 21
Can I have some mash?

Today I sit in my messy lounge, throws thrown about, a washing basket piled up with freshly ironed clothes courtesy of Millie. The sun is shining brightly down on the foliage that I can see as I look down the length of my house, through the kitchen and out of the window to the garden. I am the author of proceedings as I sit with my feet up with my laptop and beautiful 11-month-old puppy Solomon sharing my sofa. Life is good. So why do I so often look for things to wreck it? I am not really a misery, but I have started to become a bit of a menopausal moaner. It is not good progress, even if I have changed from a cup-throwing, door-slamming, screaming banshee.

Rest brings up feelings of guilt, which is pretty stupid really, as I am currently post-surgery and also I work hard most of the time.

> Leave here, turn eastward and hide in the Kerith Ravine, east of the Jordan. You will drink from the brook, and I have instructed the ravens to supply you with food there.
> *1 Kings 17:3-4*

Elijah is told to rest by God. Then again in 1 Kings 19:5: 'Then he lay down under the bush and fell asleep. All at once an angel touched him and said, "Get up and eat."'

Sometimes God ordains that we should rest; He has His reasons, and we need to be obedient and allow ourselves to experience His care. Then, like Elijah, we might hear His still, quiet voice. I often tell my clients that the word 'rest' is a verb – a doing word!

So, today, I am determined to enjoy the moment, despite the mess, despite the fact that I am missing a fabulous church day out. It is about choosing, choosing the right choice. So peeling the potatoes is my choice right now… is that resting?

***

Four days later and I have done relatively well with the keeping calm thing as long as I am in control. Now, I am sure many of you are mothers, and even if you are not, then you are daughters, so you will understand that desire of mine to remain in control, and I don't just mean of myself but also of my children and my parents.

I am a woman of 52, so you can imagine my children are growing up fast (I was a late starter). It is so hard, especially when your daughter is walking a certain path and you are desperate that she does not. I have battled and cried and shouted (at God!) and have discovered that I cannot do it for her. I am a bit of a slow learner, I know; it's not just that learning is hard, it is also hard to trust God in these circumstances; they feel so big and because I have always been a survivor and have survived on my wits and no one else's, when it all goes wrong I revert to type and go into survivor mode from old.

I remember an incident with my husband. A number of years ago, he challenged me about which account my wages were paid into. Standing at the sink in my bedroom with my back to him, he asked me. When I told him that they were paid into a separate account, he challenged me. I can clearly recall the anxiety I felt at the idea that they should be paid it into the shared account. Now, this was not because I kept the money for myself, because I didn't – it went into the family expenses, the same as his wages did. But the idea that I would not have something put aside that I was in sole control of sent me into a spiralling panic. I needed to look after myself just in case; but why, and in case of what? I was married to a faithful man and I had been faithful, too, but I could not shake off that feeling that I might need to resort to my old pattern. It was like time stood still as I considered my dilemma. Looking at my own face in the mirror, God challenged me and so I uttered those freeing words, 'I will ask work to pay it into the other account.'

Now I am aware that this does not sound like much of a big deal, but it was – I was breaking with one of my old patterns, and it really made a difference to me, and also probably to my marriage too.

***

So back to today and trusting God with my daughter: a different issue but one that still carries a similar weight. So how do we do that? I am a very protective woman, even more so with my children. Will God protect her? Does He love her as much as I do? Well, He made her so He must do. But how do we let go and still love? When I let go I sometimes withdraw, and I don't want to do that. So I pray, 'Lord, please look after my daughter; please protect her and stop her from walking away from her faith. Please help me to be a mother full of wisdom and love. Amen.'

I am a great believer in honesty, and sharing common issues has always been a great encouragement, so I pray that you are encouraged as I share mine.

It's the end of the day and I am battling not to take it back from God. When I do, I start to experience rage – it rises up in me and almost seems to threaten my sanity. I know that sounds very over the top, but my rage mixed with frustration is a very volatile combination. However, having risen up it is slowly subsiding, thank goodness, and I can breathe easily again. A bit of a close run thing, though.

Being a woman of God is so hard.

As the woman of leisure that I am at the moment, I am able to share with you the lovely lessons that I have time to receive from God. I think I will call them 'Lessons from the sofa'.

In the book *The Sacred Romance* by John Eldredge, I have discovered the words that describe that thing that happens when you try to be still with God and your mind is all over the place: 'Ontological lightness'. It is the condition that reveals that when I stop 'doing' and simply listen to my heart, I am not anchored in anything substantive. I become aware that my very identity is synonymous with activity. My soul reacts like a feather in the afternoon breeze, flitting from place to place without any direction or purpose. It is common to us all.

I love words that explain the conditions that are familiar to us all, as they normalise and ground me.

So much for lessons from a sofa. I have just started work again even though my leg is still not in a walking plaster. It was slightly hairy – the walking conditions, not my leg, I mean! It started to rain during the last session and I have a very slight slope to walk down when I leave my room, and the slabs are smooth and have a slightly mossy look to them. But I survived and am here to tell the tale.

The trouble with going back to work is that it distracts me from God, but that is the usual way we live, so it is about stealing moments with Him, isn't it, or better still perfecting the art of being aware of His presence as we walk through our day, but how?

As a counsellor, I try to listen to God and to my client, and I sometimes hear God's voice after I have already made a wrong comment that is based on my concern for the individual. Then God allows me to know that He cares and that I need not worry so much. I know that it is much better to rest in Him, and then my response will be faith based rather than fear based. So as I sit in a café, I am trying to hear Him as I edit my writing, and I am still learning the lessons written here, but in this very moment I have found a place of calm and am aware of His arms holding me as I attempt this task He has asked me to do.

***

Here is something I learnt about fear and faith that came from a talk by neuroscientist Dr Caroline Leaf. She said that within the brain, in the free will part, we have the opportunity to respond to any outside stimuli in a fearful way or a faith-filled way.[1]

A friend of mine and I have decided that we will try to be biblically under the authority of our husbands, which is no mean feat when we are both controlling. I was doing well until I didn't like the way he was doing things! Take parenting, for example – I decided that I would ask him to become more active and even take over to some degree the homework and generally 'staying on the case' role for our 12-year-old son.

David accepted and all was well, until the second night when my son played second fiddle to the computer. This is what sometimes happens with me and I feel ignored, and this morning I have totally lost it. I will not tell you what terrible words have emanated from my lips. My only saving grace is that I was really challenged in my spirit and eventually replayed the events and saw very clearly my part in it all. I was trying to take control because I did not like what I was seeing, when really no harm would have happened (or nothing major anyway) if I had just let things run their course. The trouble is, if I don't do anything, I believe that I am letting my son down and being a rubbish mother, when in fact I am failing anyway because I am not letting him take responsibility. Does this ring any bells with you?

---

[1] Caroline Leaf, *Who switched off my brain?* Published in 2008 by Switch off your brain USA Inc.

Anyway, sorry really is the hardest word, but we often feel better once we have said it.

***

Life has just gone crazy again… I have been walking past the room not spending much time with my heavenly Father. How does that happen?

Today Bonnie leaves home to work in London for a charity. I thought it would be ok, but as I sit here alone I am overwhelmed with memories of playing with her, laying on the bed in the hospital just hours after giving birth and looking into her beautiful eyes. And now I am aware of time: where did it go? I want it back. The little girl who looked up at me now looks *at* me. I am not her 'be all' any more, and it is so hard. Of course, I want her to go and do all the things God has in store for her. And honestly, I will not miss the yogurt pots with spoons in left around the house, or her bag on the table or the way I can tell exactly where she has been… But I will miss seeing her keys on the stairs that let me know she is home. I will miss her smiling at me and saying, 'I love you, Mum.' I want the years back, but I can't have them, so now I really have to rely on my Father to help me do this thing today. He knows what it is like when His children leave home; He can help me.

Today I discovered the power of hatred. That is probably too strong a word, but it was definitely an extreme feeling of hurt and confusion that resulted in me feeling totally defended and unforgiving. I had been verbally maligned and felt the searing burn of injustice. How did Jesus manage? I had not done what I had been accused of; it was unfair and untrue. However, as I tried to focus on blessing this morning, I discovered that these awful feelings were running around my head vying for attention; I had kept the offending text messages on my phone just in case I needed the evidence, when suddenly I knew I had to delete them, so I did; the relief was instantaneous. I had let go. I no longer had the evidence to fuel my anger and so I then forgave the person concerned.

That sounds terribly spiritual, doesn't it, but when you consider that I had spoken about the offending messages to a number of friends I don't look so good, do I? But anyway, I am free now, and I am suddenly aware of my head being able to focus again.

***

Feeling frazzled again, it seems like I am often like this. It is not good. Today I had a window in my day where I had the opportunity to clean out the fish tank, so I listened to Joyce Meyer at the same time. She talked about listening to God and not being reactive but waiting and listening. But I am reactive and often react without waiting for guidance. As I cleaned the tank, God spoke into my life: 'You sometimes live as someone who looks through green sludge and does not take the time to clean out your tank.'

It is often the simple messages that resound so loud in our inner being!

***

Weeks are flying by and this book is proving to be particularly elusive. I have been ill on and off since the summer and I just don't seem to be really better. I have had blood tests and antibiotics, just in case, but today I still feel like there is something stuck in my throat. To be totally honest, I am a bit afraid that I may be depressed or on the edge of something.

So how do we stop our thoughts distracting our days and making them miserable? How can our positive selves disappear and leave in their wake a flat, unenergetic wreck?

'Know who you are.' The words seem to appear like writing on the wall. So who am I? Sometimes I really don't know. We are the sum of all our parts – the good, the bad and the ugly.

The past and the present in some way lead us into the future and define us. Does this change if you are a Christian? Well, it can do, if we let God into those areas: we can experience a rewriting of the past, or rather the power of the past is diminished and thus rewritten.

So if we are to discover who we are, then I imagine that we will need to seek God and see what He says. As I sit here typing, the sky has darkened and the rain has started to fall, and there amongst it all God has placed a rainbow. I suppose we can say that knowing who we are will release the rainbow in our lives. We can then see the faint colours that He will add as we give Him permission to drive the darks clouds away. So what are the clouds that darken my horizon? Are they the same as yours?

One of mine is age, and a sense of not wanting to get it wrong now that I am nearer to 60 than 40. I don't want to live my life full of fear, but want to live it full of joy in the moment.

Here is a moment of today: walking in the teeming rain with my dogs, a five-month-old black lab cross, Mabel, who I bought myself for my birthday, and a 15-month-old brown lab cross, Solomon, and my fabulous and funny daughter Millie. I love those moments as we walk in silence, then a funny memory is recalled and we both crack up laughing. Or when I wonder aloud why she would think that purple tights and a mini skirt is the correct garb for walking dogs in a wood, on a wet and windy day in November, and she replies that she likes to wear them. I love the way the woods change depending on where you focus. As the aforementioned older woman I have the privilege of wearing varifocals so I have to look at where I walk in case I fall over!

***

I have just popped round to my friend's house to sit with her dog for a while (my friend was out, by the way!). While I was there I flicked through her TV channels and came upon *Extreme Makeover*. This programme is not for the faint-hearted as it shows facial surgery. Anyway, there I am watching two women getting rid of aspects of themselves that I also do not like about myself – jowls in my case.

It was strange, really. To be honest, I would like to get rid of my jowls, but as I watched and listened I was aware that both of these women's self-worth was based on what they looked like. I also fluctuate between feeling positive about what I looked like and feeling rubbish.

I am blessed to have three beautiful daughters, and when I say beautiful I mean that; but it is also hard to see their beauty reflected in my fading glory. Anyway, as the last shot of the newly made-over women faded from the screen, I am sure that I heard God whisper that He does not look at outside beauty but at the internal self.

***

I have finally come back up from what seems to be a very long haul of intermittent illness. I feel as though I have been in a very dark place, where it is hard to work out where your body's pain and mind's torment end and begin. What I mean is that I have had a constant feeling of being under the weather while my mind has plagued me that I am making it up. So I am out of the bad mind stuff and now have entered another stage – one where I am lying about the place with pins sticking out of my toes: the result of more surgery to put right what didn't work the first time round!

Does it mean when something does not go according to plan that we have stepped out of God's will?

I don't know the answer, but I don't think that God has moved away; I am just aware that He uses everything in our lives to talk to us: blessings, illness, hardships, any circumstances that we find ourselves in. So what is He saying to me at this time?

Well, I am more aware than ever how stroppy I can get, and really about nothing. Let's take the potato situation.

'Anything you want me to do when I get home?' David asked as we left church.

My usual response would be, 'Nothing, everything is done,' but that day was different and he had said the day before, 'Don't worry about doing a roast dinner – have a rest.'

Now I am a bit of a traditionalist and have cooked Sunday lunch for the past 20 years, but I had planned bangers and mash as an alternative.

'Can you do some potato for mash?' I asked. He looked surprised but agreed.

On our return I started to prepare the leeks and carrots that I was going to mash with them when my daughter told me that David was making roast potatoes. It is ridiculous, but I threw a strop, and the confrontation started.

It was crazy. He made roast; I made mash.

'Can I have some of your veg?'

'No, I need it for my mash.'

I proceeded to make yummy mash and he made delicious roast. Finally the serving time arrived and I was still determined to remain in charge, and cross.

'I will swap you some roast for some mash,' he said with a smile on his face.

I turned away slightly so that he could not see the smile that was starting to play about my face in the most annoying fashion. I did not want to step back from my position. It was almost like it had become comfortable to be angry, or at least so familiar that I could not be another way, but finally I did crack. I really cannot believe that I got so cross about nothing.

Another opportunity to confess my foolishness:

Take the new coffee jars that I bought a few years ago. There they were, with brightly coloured spots and stripes – one for coffee, one for tea and one for sugar. I was happy to work out which one was which but David had other ideas and stuck on labels when I wasn't looking. I went bonkers.

'You can't put them on there! That ruins them.'

Let me tell you, I was completely serious and a row started that did not end for ages. I cannot believe I was so ridiculous, but I was.

What is God teaching me as I think back? One thing for sure is that I get stressed about very silly things. Why do some things take on such importance? Surely there are more important things in life? I think it is about control and feeling put down and not valued enough. Is my self-worth so fragile? If it is, why is that? I am going to try and check it out, so watch this space. I am just hoping that I don't turn out to be a spoilt child…

Chapter 22
Prepared to pay the price?

I am spoilt. Are you?

We live, and here I am speaking to those who live in relative luxury in the West, often focused on ourselves, our wants, our perceived needs and our need to look a certain way. It is Christmas soon and because of my foot surgery I have had to get everything sorted before December has even started. I planned that I would only spend a limited budget on my children, but as usual that has gone out of the window with me saying the same old thing, 'I am buying them things they need, not expensive luxuries...'!

Now I have always said that I am a content woman who does not hanker after expensive things. I do not even know the names of many designers, and this is something that I like about myself. But this Christmas I saw a photograph in a shop window for a watch made by Links of London. Friends of mine have been sporting their bracelets and necklaces for a while; if they had not, I would not have known what they were. So anyway, I saw this advertisement and my friend and I both said we would ask our respective husbands for one for Christmas. Now those who know me know that once I get an idea in my head I do not put it down easily. So first of all I primed my husband, who also is not into designer things and would go for a cheaper alternative.

'David, I would really like one of those watches that are in blah blah. You could go shopping with Millie...' On and on I went.

Then I started to look on the internet: £200 to £300! Well, I know that David loves me and I did get a diamond ring a few years back to replace the ring he had given me 18 years previously, but I could not imagine him spending that at the moment.

The thing that confuses me is how and why does something that just tells you the time and prevents you being early or points out when you are late get such a high value? Why does it mean that you are a special person? Why do certain labels, name tags, styles, etc mean so much?

God does say that man looks at the outside appearance but that He (God) looks at the heart. So how did this way of thinking start in the first place?

So back to the hunt for the watch, I could not agree that paying that much was ok. So I start to look for another watch that was individual but stylish. Anyway, the long and short of it was that I found one and told my husband, who then found it cheaper somewhere else! 'Have you looked at these?' he said. I went in the other room to peer over his shoulder at the screen. Now, often I get upset and confuse his caution with meanness, but this time I did not and what followed was a few hours of fun as we sat side by side and found the original watch that I had wanted, in a sale and at a massively reduced price. We bought it, and a ring, for a fraction of the original price, and then spent the rest of the evening sitting together watching a programme on television. It was so lovely.

Now why have I told you all about this?

Well, I have been wondering, as I said previously, about why things that we acquire take on such meaning? Is it a form of worship, a kind of golden calf? I think it is. The Israelites built themselves a golden calf to worship instead of God, and thus they lost their focus on God.

1 Timothy 6:6–7 says:

Godliness with contentment is great gain. For we brought nothing into the world, and we can take nothing out of it. But if we have food and clothing, we will be content with that. Those who want to get rich fall into temptation and a trap and into many foolish and harmful desires that plunge people into ruin and destruction. For the love of money is a root of all kinds of evil. Some people, eager for money, have wandered from the faith and pierced themselves with many griefs.

So here I sit, having spent too much money on presents and pondering on these verses.

When we live in a culture of debt, do we wander away from God and get pierced with many upsets?

I know that after Christmas, children that are counselled in our agency, and many who are not experience the pain of seeing the toys that they have been given being sent back to the shops. This is because many parents get caught up in the Christmas frenzy of buying beyond their financial means. In addition, their parents become anxious or aggressive due to the burden of debts that they cannot cover.

Why do we need to have so many things to feel good? I understand that parents want to lavish good things on their children. I do it. The Bible even talks about it:

Which of you, if your son asked for bread, will give him a stone? Or if he asks for a fish, will give him a snake? If you, then, though you are evil, know how to give good gifts to your children, how much more will your Father in heaven give good gifts to those who ask him!
Matthew 7:9-11

But we want so much for ourselves as well. We have become the 'want it now' generation.

I had a magazine arrive today – Joyce Meyer's magazine – and, as I am still not back to work full-time, I have the space to read it. 'Dreams are not free... what are you willing to pay?' said an article:

Have you ever walked through a shopping mall or car lot when POW; THE perfect product catches you attention?... dress... car...

Honestly – talk about perfect timing;! It goes on to talk about the price we have to pay for the dream and how all dreams begin obstacle free but in the end we have to be willing to pay the price of the dream.

Am I prepared to pay the price? Are you?

Actually, I am not. I know I have spent too much at Christmas and that we will have to sort out our accounts: the idea of paying for something over the long term that then proceeds to deteriorate before we have finished paying is not my idea of fun.

What about things that we aspire to do? The dreams we dream affect our families and could lead us to compromising our beliefs and the things that we value.

And what about God, and my relationship with Him? Am I prepared to pay the price for the dream? Having a close relationship, one where I spend time with Him, enough time that I can recognise His voice when He speaks, is so important, but I so often sacrifice it for other desires.

***

What a week. Does it ever get easy? I thought that the no-alcohol thing would be a walk in the park. No such luck. I have really struggled with all the advertising for Christmas drinks that are out there to entice us to celebrate in a certain way. As I have watched them, and now I can confess that I have watched them too much – too much TV in my life again – I have felt miserable. It is not good feeling like that, and then yesterday, after spending the morning shopping again, I was left with the feeling that I had taken my eyes off God. Add to that just for good measure a lovely evening of contemporary worship where God turns up and challenges me and loves me.

So I awake today with a new determination to focus on Him instead of the drink that sparkles in the glass. My cynical side wants to say, 'And how long will that last?' A phone call regarding my father threatens to send me spiralling down, but I am going to hold tight to my God and focus on Him.

***

My dad has had a stroke and I have been thrown into close contact with him and his girlfriend. This has been a challenge, I want to say, but in fact it has not been too bad. It appears that God has demolished my rage against the two of them and I am now able to stay in the room with them. I think really what has happened is that I am now no longer holding my mother's grief and anger, holding on to that rescuing feeling that keeps me constantly in a state of high alert for danger. I have had to let go and allow her to feel her own feelings and not take on hers as well as mine. Now that does not mean I don't care; of course I do, and I still get anxious and still challenge as much as ever, but I am only doing it with my own feelings to the forefront.

Talking of feelings, my foot hurts so much. Yesterday they pulled out the pins from my toes without any pain relief. It was truly awful and today I feel vulnerable, and my toe is so painful that I have come home from work having seen the children I work with for only a very short session. One lovely little boy, seeing my pain when I walked, pulled my arm around his shoulder and instructed me to lean on him and other objects to help me – so precious, so kind.

Now I am home on the sofa with my foot elevated. Once again I am thinking that I really should call this book *Musings from a sofa* as it is really the only time that I get a chance to write. Or do I write only when I am too ill to do anything else?

***

It is now 2010. Oh my goodness, the last few weeks have been a roller coaster of emotions as I have picked up and put down rage, and now I feel calm again. The calm has come because I have confronted Dad's girlfriend and demanded that she tell the truth. I have spoken to Dad as well and now I am no longer the colluder of secrets; I cannot tolerate deception and have to speak out. I am no hero but I am a woman of integrity.

So it's a new year, a new start and I am excited and challenged. I am challenged about how to love my lovely husband with *phileo* love (a Greek word from the Bible that means a generous, affectionate , warm love). I am, as usual reading many books: one for the Jane Austen book club – very exciting – and *Feminine Appeal* by Carolyn Mahaney, which has challenged my love walk. The challenge is to respect and enjoy our husbands with a tender affectionate love. I love the idea of it but other things get in the way, like parents and children and work. So crazy when you think that he is the main man in my life and I take it and him for granted. So 2010 is going to be the year when I try not to overload and to spend some time with him! (I wish you could see the wry smile that has appeared as I write this.)

Chapter 23
I am grumpy

Are you like me? When life seems to ease up do you have the urge to make things harder, almost as if you are afraid of skiving off, thinking that only when you are struggling are you really working hard enough?

How do we know with all certainty that we are loved in a lavish way? If we did know, then surely our whole approach to life would have a different tension to it; a kind of gentle approach to ourselves and others that often appears elusive. Well, it does to me anyway.

So 'love' – what does that look like? I reckon it is a deep knowledge that only increases in awareness when you spend time with the 'love giver'. It really is a kind of romance where you listen to each other and look at each other, and pay attention to each other's needs. A bit like me and my son: he is into computer games that do not excite me and do not attract me but if, like right now, I sit with him and let him teach me about what he loves to do, I find a new interest and joy in the room as he delights to tell me new things. Now I have to say that I am only interested in these things at this moment because he is, and I am spending time with him, and I love him. So I asked him what he thinks about me spending time with him.

'To be honest I just like being with you. I like doing stuff with you,' he said. What a lovely thing to be told.

I wonder if God feels like that. Is He only interested in certain things because we are? And vice versa, are we interested in what God is interested in only when we spend time with Him and He shows us new things that we did not know before?

We are made in His image, after all, and so we reflect His nature in what we love receiving from a relationship – godly things, I mean. To really know my son and what he loves will only truly happen when I give him space and time to talk to me. Time to hear the little things that take time to hear, opportunity for space for wonderings and musings to share treasures and secret desires; in fact, today I was challenged to spend larger amounts of time with God.

Have you ever thought of going on a guided retreat for a day, or preferably longer? It sounds like a luxury but really, if you want to grow in any relationship, you need to spend time with that person. I have been to a number of weddings where the vicar talked about how necessary it is for a successful marriage to spend time with your partner. The truth is the same about time spent with God.

***

Now I am down in the dumps; I have argued and cried. My ear infection has got worse and I have had to go to the GP again this morning and have been given more medication. Yesterday I was ill. Jarv (my pet name for David) had to go for a foot X-ray as he had badly twisted his ankle. (Not sure if it was 'man-foot'! Ha-ha.) In fact, it turned out to be ok. Then two of my daughters were both ill. I just couldn't believe it – every day bar one this week I have had one or more children off sick – not the best environment to spend time alone with God, but also just part of life and mothering. They couldn't help it; they didn't *want* to be ill.

Anyway, feeling so low, taking my time I finally read my Bible notes and, surprise, surprise, God spoke into my life:

We do not know what we ought to pray for, but the Spirit himself intercedes for us through wordless groans.
Romans 8:26

So today has become a day of exhaustion and sighing, a day when I finally gave myself permission to be ill.

I ended up spending the weekend constantly cross with David; I felt let down by him and unloved by him. It was all because he appeared reluctant to help me do the tasks I normally do without giving a second thought. And today I was going down the same road, until I spoke to a friend early in the day and we recognised how the enemy distracts us into a pattern of criticism and so all we can see are the things that annoy us.

So we agreed that I would have a day of expectation, where I would focus on the things of God instead of negative things. Ok, it was not all plain sailing; I had planned to spend a large amount of time alone with God, but one of my children was at home which meant that I eventually sat down with God and my Bible after lunch. But you know, because I had started the day with a better focus, I went through my day with a better attitude. I enjoyed doing tasks and talking to my daughter – not that I don't normally, but when you are unwell it can be difficult. Everything about the day was better – my eyes were more aware of good things, and when I had some time sitting with God I was able to hear what He was saying in a better manner.

In *A New Kind of Christian*, Brian D McClaren talks about how we should show we are Christians by being 'good'. The question then is what does 'goodness' look like? And how can our goodness point others to Jesus? I mean, there are plenty of 'good' people out there.

Is goodness about being like Jesus? The Bible says that no one is good, only God, so where does that leave us?

'Why do you ask me about what is good?' Jesus replied.
'There is only One who is good. If you want to enter life,
keep the commandments.'
Matthew 19:17

So I suppose that means we need to try and be like our
Father. And how do we do that, apart from spending time
with our Father in order to become more like Him, to hear
what He is saying and to hear what He is thinking about? So I
go back again to what I discovered just last week. Time spent
with God is always the best investment, and only investment
brings dividends.

Which brings me nicely to my marriage; it is in real need of
investment, and today the challenge arrived in the form of a
book called *The Love Dare* by Stephen and Alex Kendrick,
which focuses on treating our husband/wife in an honouring
manner. How challenging that is, especially when I have been
focusing on negative thoughts. If all goes according to plan,
David won't know what has hit him. The plan is to wait until
the book arrives and start it as a journey through Lent. It takes
40 days and so will be my act of worship. However, I am
hoping to start now, and I have to say, so far so good today,
but you know what it's like now: I always want recognition for
the good that I do, I crave words of affirmation, I struggle with
defensive anger when I feel unjustly treated. It doesn't look
that likely that I will succeed, and on my own I won't; I will
need to get help from my Father and know that He sees what I
do and feels my disappointments and defends me against
accusation. I need to make sure that I listen to the Father of
heavenly lights.

Every good and perfect gift is from above, coming down
from the Father of the heavenly lights, who does not
change like shifting shadows.
James 1:17

So I reckon that He can help me do this. He has, after all, given me the good intentions necessary to be focused on my marriage.

***

Life at home is ok – normal stuff apart from the fact that I am still not working, my ear is still deaf and I still have one foot bandaged up, which means that I have one unbandaged foot!! Hooray, one foot now looks normal, and I am praying that the other one is ok.

So back to my previously asked question: do you think that when something goes wrong that you were not meant to do it in the first place? I mean, three operations on one foot just to sort out a bunion – surely that's not right? Did I not check it out with God properly, or do things like this just happen and I am over-spiritualising everything? It is so hard to work out, and I *think* that I am aware of God's voice in my life!

Take yesterday, for example. I was trying to be a good wife when I became irritated with my husband and got hurt over something he said, and then I heard God tell me to be tender. Now I don't know about you, but when I hear God I am likely to respond in a more positive manner, and the word 'tender' stopped me in my tracks.

As I reran my conversation with David through my mind, I realised that he heard a harsh edge to my voice, and not just that: I was in the habit of being harsh and I realised that I need to work on this!

God is persistent, isn't He?

Today I was reading 2 Peter 1:3–7:

His divine power has given us everything we need for a godly life through our knowledge of him who called us by his own glory and goodness. Through these he has given us his very great and precious promises, so that through them you may participate in the divine nature, having escaped the corruption in the world caused by evil desires. For this reason, make every effort to add to your faith goodness; and to goodness, knowledge; and to knowledge, self-control; and to self-control, perseverance; and to perseverance, godliness; and to godliness, mutual affection; and to mutual affection, love.

The list went on, and as I read I realised that there is a natural rhythm, but also that I was at the beginning needing to be good, which was what I was talking about the other day!

So life is developing into a constant challenge, a challenge of being the woman of God that I am meant to be, regardless of how others behave.

The other day my husband and I completed a test about how we operate in the world; the results were interesting for both of us, particularly me. It confirmed some thoughts I had been having and went a good way towards me understanding him more and probably being more compassionate. Anyway, I know now, and I am going to use this knowledge to try and understand him more.

Chapter 24
Zimmer throwing

It's the beginning of another week and I notice that the counting of weeks has gone out of the window.

How come God does not let us off the hook?

It can't just be me, can it?

One minute it is, 'Be tender to him.'

And the next it is, 'Keep strife out of your life!'

God keeps having to point things out to me. Now this means either that I am a bit dense or that I am a work in progress. I don't hear God's voice as condemning, thank goodness. In fact, if I do feel crushed or put down I should recognise the voice of the enemy – still haven't quite got that bit sorted...

So, yes the strife bit. I was getting irritated by my husband AGAIN and God butted in via some old Bible notes that had surfaced from under my bed, when I had a rare 'sort it all out' moment. The notes said something like, 'strife was designed especially to mess up marriages'. Now that made sense to me. Do nothing out of selfish ambition or vain conceit. Rather, in humility value others above yourselves.
Philippians 2:3

So, what else will I discover as I endeavour to be a woman of God?

We agreed to not 'do' Valentine's Day, but I was still disappointed that he did not give me a card, and because we agreed not to do anything I did not give him the card I had bought him. We ended up having a fairly miserable day, where he upset me and I sulked the rest of the time feeling unable to move on from what he had said. I did cook him a very nice curry for when he returned from church though; it was, of course, a breakdown in communication that caused the upset. Post-operation blues are pursuing me...

Haircut dilemma: I have always been a spur of the moment sort of person, and that includes the area of haircuts which have been mainly short and spiky in varying colours for a number of years. So last week I decided that I needed to have a haircut to cheer myself up, but, being a dutiful wife, I decided that I would keep it on the long side as David likes it longer – see I am trying! Once done I returned home and walked into the front room to ask whether he liked it or not. He said, 'Hello, Bob.'

I was not best pleased, as I am sure you can imagine. It was rather boring, I suppose, and was a sort of 'Bob' hairstyle, which was confirmed by his response. Still I decided to leave it as it was, until the next day when my friend came round and said that she liked it – it was 'neat'.

'Neat!' I shrieked. 'You mean, like Lego hair?'

'No, it's more like Playmobil hair,' she laughed.

'That's it,' I cried. 'Where's the phone book? I am having it all chopped off,' and that is what I did.

So now I am the proud owner of a short, spiky haircut that I like, and so does everyone apart from David, but I figure that if I like the way I look, I will feel better about myself and he will benefit from my better mood. So with my new haircut I have joined Weight Watchers and am about to embark on the *Love Dare*: blimey, I don't give myself a break, do I?

***

Typical! I wake with earache, still. I am feeling terrible and I am reduced to tears as I realise that I am not getting better. I

142

thought that I would be taken out today (I still can't drive) and the sun is shining, the sky is a brilliant blue – and I feel totally wrung out, my head feels like it is really heavy. In fact, I am typing at a very weird angle with my head flopped sideways on the sofa. The question is, does Satan turn up with the other angels before God and does God say, 'Have you checked out Susie? She is fab,' etc (like it says in Job 2:3: 'Then the Lord said to Satan, "Have you considered my servant Job?"') – you know what I mean – and then does he come and have a pop? I do feel somewhat pursued, I have to say. One thing's for sure, I will find out what is what in due time.

Same day, midnight. I am sitting watching the Vancouver winter Olympics and it is the curling competition. I have never watched it before, just caught snippets of it and thought of it as a rather strange sport. But it is intriguing me tonight. Turns are taken by various members of the team to push a polished block of granite along the surface to a target with the aim of pushing the other competitor's blocks off the target to gain the central position.

What is really interesting is the guy who pushes the granite stone has two or three sweepers who frantically push their brooms in front of the granite to keep it moving. He cannot do it alone. As I watched, I realised how like the Christian walk it is. Take today, for example: I have felt awful and friends have been praying for me to keep me going. I in turn am praying for a friend who is really struggling. As we pray, we sweep away the grit and stuff that can cause us to stumble, and so the person who succeeds – me today – only gets through it because they are faithfully covered when they cannot do it alone.

***

Life is so hard; I am still unwell and am sick of my moaning voice. Tomorrow I am going on Premier Radio to be interviewed by Jeff Lucas and Ruth Dearnley, which is great. I can tell them about my book, but I feel down and poorly. God will need to hold me up in order for me to do this thing, although I am sure that adrenaline will also help me.

Remember that *Love Dare* book? Well, I am doing it, but it is not going too well. I am ill and so am unable to do the dares very effectively. Now the question is, should I give myself a break, as my sister asked me this morning?

'The osteopath told you to take things easy. Do you think that you should be giving yourself another thing to do?'

The thing is, when I set myself a challenge I want to finish it, but I am very good at not seeing things through too. Half-read books litter my house. Will this be another one? Come to think of it, the things I don't complete are often the things that are about investing in me. And they are also about attainment, me trying to improve myself. How to pray better, be a better Christian... They all give the possibility of failure, which it feels as though I do at every turn. Why does it have to be such hard work? Is that the life Jesus meant when He said we would have life to the full?

***

I have just watched *Secret Millionaire* where Dawn, a millionaire, helped various organisations who support drug addicts and alcoholics and prostitutes. It really challenged me. I was once addicted and, although I was not a prostitute, I did give my body for drugs. How far has God changed me; how did He manage that?

The other weekend I went to a Faith Works conference and one of the speakers, Jeff Lucas again, told the story of the prodigal son with some added information that I had not known before. He said that when prodigals returned home, the village would race out to meet the offender and they would get a jar of spices and nuts and break it, to signify that the village wanted nothing more to do with them. Therefore, when the father saw his son a long way off he ran (most undignified for a man then), and staged a party of welcome to prevent the 'Kazaza' from taking place.

When I think of God's redeeming love, it is the same: He runs to us, He runs to us to prevent us being permanently banned from town, or family or society.

It is strange that watching the *Secret Millionaire* has lifted my spirits. To remember where you have come from can make all the difference. So my Father, our Father, can reach out to us and catch us when we are in dire danger of falling too far.

***

I HAVE PLUMMETED DOWN AN EMOTIONAL RAVINE THAT HAS TAKEN ME TO A PLACE I HAVE NEVER BEEN BEFORE. I am exhausted, wrung out, despairing and feel young, so very young. I have totally lost my temper.

My dad lived in a nursing home after his stroke because he was unable to look after himself. He would not let my mother help him as he wanted to be with another woman. That resulted in him being very alone because he had chosen her over us all: his children, grandchildren and the rest of the family.

My sister had told me that he was saying that no one loved him. He was feeling lonely and his girlfriend had stopped visiting him so much. So, typical of me, I decided to try and make him feel better by visiting him in my lunch hour. As I drove there I prayed that it would be ok and that I would not react to him, but my plan was to utterly fail. This is how the visit went:

'Oh it's you, I thought Mandy was coming.'

'Oh, a nice surprise then,' I say as I bend to kiss the proffered cheek.

'How are you?'

'Terrible, bored.'

I sit on the bed and try to think of something that I can say that won't be contentious.

'Can you move that picture?' he asks, pointing to the drawing of the woman he is having his strange relationship with, the woman that I have had major fallings-out with.

I proceed to move it six inches to the left as requested.

'Can you pass me the photographs on the window sill too?'

Again I pick up more pictures of her and hand them to him. I sit there watching as he tries to adjust the frame. Eventually he hands it back to me and asks me to place it back on the window sill.

As he asks me how my feet are, my heart flickers with the unbidden thought that he remembers me and is asking after me. However, that was not to last, and as he starts to moan about my lovely sister not doing some task, I leap to her defence and it starts to go downhill.

He starts to talk about not getting out enough, which results in me suggesting that if I bring my children in to see him, he should refrain from talking about his 'woman'.

'I am not going to abide by your rules,' he shouts.

'Fine, I just won't bring them in.'

The conversation starts to plummet downhill fast, and before long he is shouting at me that I am not 'God's gift'.

'I know that,' I shout back at him, by now in a child place. 'All I want is for you to be tender to me.'

'Tender! I am not going to crawl all over you,' he sneers. 'Are you getting upset now?' he continues cruelly.

And I shout at him. 'Anyone would think I am a hard-nosed woman.'

'You are. You always have been,' is his response.

My rage has now risen and threatens to overwhelm me. His condemnation is so painful. What started out as me not wanting him to be lonely has once again resulted in breakdown. Why was I so stupid to think it could be any different? Putting my face inches from him I scream, 'You have voted with your feet and chosen her,' as I point to the picture he had asked me to move just minutes before.

It is around that time that my sister arrives, to a scene of growing rage. She tries to manhandle me out of the room but his comments have resulted in me fighting my corner like a wild cat.

'Come on then,' I shout, beckoning to him as I return to the room after he called me a 'bloody bitch'.

'Give me your worst.'

'I never want to see you again,' he shouts.

'Fine,' I scream back, and throw his walking frame towards him.

My sister manages to deflect the frame and shouts at me, 'Enough!'

And she pulls me out of the room.

***

I am exhausted just recalling that time. I wanted to grind my heel into the picture of the woman that he had abandoned his family for. I was enraged and broken and shocked that I could still feel so deeply the pain of his words. I felt like a little girl again, and I knew that I needed help.

Many things have happened since then that have helped me recognise that I have reached a crossroads on my journey. Now I have to finally confront the rage and let my inner child have some space and love and nurture. It feels like the visit happened weeks ago, but it has only been six days!

In a very sorry state, I eventually made it back to the office and to my much-loved friend Liz. I finally told her and went on to recall the whole chaotic mess.

'If you did not do rage, what would you do?' she asked.

After some thought the word 'despair' finally came to mind.

'Despair, and I don't do that. There is no hope in despair.'

'I think the time has come to find a therapist that I can feel safe with,' I uttered, and she agreed.

Later that week I was invited to London to hear Rob Bell speak. It was a brilliant evening, but the key point for me was when he invited us all to write on the pieces of white card that were situated on our seats the words 'I know how you feel'.

We were to write in our non-dominant hand.

He then invited us to hold up our card if we had known someone die.

'Look around and exchange your card with someone.' Wow, so many were no longer alone. He continued until he said, 'Put up your hand if you have been an addict.' Oh no, I will be the only one. My thoughts ricocheted around my head, but as I looked around there were too many people to count; it was really humbling. My sister told me later that he had actually said if you were an addict or had been affected by addiction in any way; Mandy had, of course, also put up her hand, but I did not know where she was sitting.

Later that same week, I went to a women's breakfast to hear a very dear friend of mine speak. As she described her life and the putting down and picking up of various suitcases of varying sizes, all full of burdens, I was aware of the prompting of God.

'He threw the suitcases down the mountain side, didn't he?' Yes, that is what my father had done on a holiday when I was a teenager, enraged that the car had broken down. Now I was going to retrieve them, metaphorically speaking, and so decide with care which ones were mine to carry. I also recognised a new slant on my story; a new title was revealed, and a slightly different slant on the previously told story:

'The 13-year-old girl picked up the walking frame in rage. As it was thrown across the room, her younger sister protected her father. The 13-year-old was sitting in her 53-year-old body.'

Potholes and belly-flops: a picture from the Lord.

I have come to a place in the cave systems and the only way forward is through the inky black pool that appears to act as a dam between where I am now and where I need to get to.

I have plunged my face into its surface many times only to remove it again, recoiling at the shock of the cold. I do not see light, only darkness, in those moments, and yet, I think if I would only plunge my entire body in, there would appear a rope that I could reach out to which would act as my guide, and as I grasped each knot, my hands would not slip. My sense is that they are perfectly shaped for my hands – small and just the right size for my child's fingers. The trouble is that it means getting wet, and I hate that – cold and wet. But dive in I must.

Because of the Lord's great love we are not consumed, for his compassions never fail. They are new every morning; great is your faithfulness. I say to myself, 'The Lord is my portion: therefore I will wait for him.'
Lamentations 3:22–24

Now 'waiting' is a verb, remember, so no lying around is required from me. Good thing, too, as I find that difficult.

Chapter 25
Not busy, fruitful

Church, the day after the breakfast, finds me still pursued and challenged.

The pastor is preaching from Colossians 3:1–14. The sermon title: 'A new way, no rage!'

As I sit next to my friend Rhoda, a written dialogue starts between us as she adds to my comments in my journal:

'There is no escape, I can't get away from rage!'

'But there is grace.'

'But I feel so angry.'

'His grace is enough even for you!'

'I know but I am being overwhelmed, knocked sideways. I think I am being judged unfairly – I just don't know any more.'

'Who is doing the judging?'

'David, my dad, anyone who disagrees with my good intentions: Hollie, Lewis…'

'And what does God say about it?'

'I don't know mostly, and then sometimes I do and then I have to confront it and then I feel guilty, and not good enough and once again I am going round in a circle that appears to pull me downwards.'

'I think this sermon was written for you…'

'Renewal.'

'There is NO condemnation in Christ Jesus even for you.'

I know that I need to deal with my rage and the way I react to others. I do feel condemned, like something is sitting on my shoulders, and I am so near to crying and not being able to stop.

Psalm 61:2: 'I call as my heart grows faint; lead me to the rock that is higher than I.'

David had some stuff to deal with too. He wrote that.

Colossians 3:9–14:

Do not lie to each other, since you have taken off your old self with its practices and have put on the new self, which is being renewed in knowledge in the image of its Creator. Here there is no Gentile or Jew, circumcised or uncircumcised, barbarian, Scythian, slave or free, but Christ is all, and is in all. Therefore, as God's chosen people, holy and dearly loved, clothe yourselves with compassion, kindness, humility, gentleness and patience. Bear with each other and forgive one another if any of you has a grievance against someone. Forgive as the Lord forgave you. And over all these virtues put on love, which binds them all together in perfect unity.

Isn't it amazing, God allows true love to dwell in the hearts of those who also hold rage, and in His tenderness He renews us. I am so grateful that He did not give up on me.

***

This is how bad it has got: yesterday my best friend asked me if I thought I might be having a nervous breakdown.

I had arrived at her house after my frantic husband had rung her to suggest that we both went out to lunch: he was paying!

After days of extremely fluctuating moods that went from tears to screaming rage, I had finally fallen apart because my unusually house-proud husband had commented that he could smell urine, after I had just told him how I had cleaned the entire bathroom on my knees and how our son had got out of the bath and trashed it, like most 13-year-old boys do. That was it for me; I lost it big time and went rapidly from swearing in his face to crying uncontrollably. How I hated myself. In the bedroom, wracked with deep sobs, I tried to think of a place that I could go. I could not think of anywhere...

I was desperate and found myself the following day at the GP saying that I thought I was depressed. I felt ashamed, but he was lovely, so kind to me. Tomorrow I go back to hear the results of the test he gave me to ascertain what I should do next – medication or not?

Prozac! Like all things at the moment, it has not been plain sailing. I had an inflamed ear when I went to the GP but she did not give antibiotics as it does not make any difference, and since then I have developed a sore throat. Last night I awoke to very bizarre thoughts. The only comparison I can give is when I had my daughter by caesarean section: they gave me a codeine-based drug and I spent the night in the nursery, planning how I would get home, as I could not hear my heart beating.

So I lay there in the darkness, planning how I would get out my laptop and sit on the floor so as not to disturb my husband and see if what I was feeling was normal. I then remembered to pray, after these crazy thoughts had assailed me for too long. I must have slept, as next thing it was morning.

But what shall I do?

'Please, Lord, help me.'

Now this is one of those moments when I am processing and so I am still unsure whether this is God's voice or my own.

So this is what is in my head: the medication does not agree with you, stop taking it and rest in God. Go somewhere where you can be still and quiet, meditate on His word or rather rest and do nothing.

About four hours later I had the most remarkable telephone call from the duty doctor whom I had never met. I rang about my concerns and she was very friendly and open. When I explained my side effects and the score on my depression scale she suggested that it may not be worth me carrying on, as the side effects would probably cancel out the benefits.

I confessed my roller coaster of rage and tears and she said that I should embrace the rage and find an outlet. When I mentioned about being a Christian, she said that Jesus had got angry and thrown people out of the Temple. She told me how she had driven to work with the top down on her car, singing very loudly, to calm herself down. I have never known a call from a doctor like it; I felt so supported, and as she recalled some more of her own antics, I asked her how she understood me. Her response was, 'I have been there.' I did wonder aloud to my friend as to whether she was a GP or an angel. I came away from that phone call a laughing, smiling woman, and the day just got better. As I sit here typing, I feel relaxed and peaceful. Long may it last!

***

Life has been interesting over the past few weeks. I have slowly recovered myself. In fact, I would almost say I have 'rediscovered' myself, that younger self that was lost in my younger years. It is strange how we live our lives shrouded in the things that are said and done to us, ensuring a life limited by the views of others.

I'm sure you're aware that most of the things said and done to me came by way of my father. To live a life blamed and shamed ensures that on some level you live exhausted in an effort to find your true self. A kind of disbelief settles on you as you seek a hope that you might be more than you were predicted to be. And you strive – yes, that is exactly what I have done. I suddenly realise that the word that was given to me on various occasions, from different sources, truly resonated with my normal way of living.

'Do not strive' originates from God's desire to free me from this subconscious desire to prove myself, to earn my father's favour.

My father's favour was not available to me. (It is now two years later and I have a better relationship with him, he loves to see me most of the time and I love to see him. The bad days are a result of the dementia that affects him.)

However, I need to know who I am in the eyes of God, despite what my earthly father thinks of me, and I think I am now nearer to understanding this than I have ever been.

I am starting to believe that my heart is good. It feels very different to even suspect that it might be true and that my heavenly Father, who knows me inside and out, could even start to show me a glimpse of this and that He believes in me and places hope in me.

So I may not be a loud-mouthed, hard-nosed woman after all; it *is* possible to regain what was lost and so be remade in a new way. So now I am embarking on a new adventure, an adventure of freedom: I am going to experiment on living life to the full. A free life, without the contamination of guilt pulling me down into the murky depths of an uncharted pothole that does not have my name on it.

Well, it has been a good week, I must say. 'Fruitful,' as Joyce Meyer would say. I am trying so hard not to use the 'busy' word: work is thrilling, I have the amazing privilege of being trusted in people's lives and seeing God use me in some amazing ways.

It is crazy that I have assumed certain things and lived in a particular way all my life, when freedom had been available all along, and I just didn't realise it. This is true for so many of us. Don't *you* think that it is crazy for a child of God to NOT know freedom? How does that happen?

I can hear myself asking God why I struggle with my thoughts; it *is* annoying that the negative words and actions from my past have overlaid my present and caused me to grow up in a particular way.

But slowly I am actually getting it. It must have been so hard for God to stand by and let these things happen, and so hard for Him to watch me flounder as I tried to understand my life.

How hard was it for God to stand by and watch the most terrible traumas that have been inflicted on the people that I work with? I really don't understand how that happened, but I do know this: many of the most traumatised people that I have the privilege of journeying with know God in their lives and are people of faith.

So, for me, freedom beckons. I have a therapeutic space to talk in and realise that my past was not my fault. I can choose to turn away finally and to live the rest of my life in a new way. That is my aim, and I believe that is God's desire for me too.

Sitting here, I realise that I am rather like a starved child, not for food but for space. Space to sit and do this, time to sit and listen out for God. Yesterday I was at the gym listening to Joyce Meyer on my headphones. It is brilliant, exercising and listening to various messages from brilliant preachers and getting physically and spiritually fit. Anyway, Joyce Meyer was talking about how we need to go through a transformation to let go of the old and take hold of the new. And she likened it to being a caterpillar, which encases itself in a cocoon, out of sight from prying eyes, where it is transformed into a butterfly. Apparently the caterpillar becomes liquid before its transformation. That picture resonated within me: does God need to do the same thing in me? Is that process trying to take place all the time but I make it all too public for Him to do it privately?

Last week I started a new training in Cognitive Behavioural Therapy (CBT). It was illuminating. I really think that many of these trainings have been taken from the Bible. So how about this: we give ourselves 'negative punishments' which keep us in the familiar negative place that we have embraced about ourselves. For me that is played out like this:

'I am fed up so I need food; I am fat so I might as well eat; my dad says I am useless so I might as well eat.'

So back to the 'negative punishment', which reflects our harsh view of ourselves and our inability to help ourselves to change in a positive, helpful way; it is almost as if we have no positive expectations so we don't need to bother. We just stay in the useless, hopeless place we are accustomed to. But if we enter the cocoon and are liquefied by God, then we will be unrecognisable... I love that picture.

I'm not sure if I told you that I am having a constant ringing in one ear, which makes it harder to hear on some level, depending on where I am. Anyway, going to bed last night, I must have asked my husband to repeat himself one too many times because he said, 'Why don't you get a couple of those discreet hearing aids that would probably help us and you?'

Ok, so another meltdown started to occur: I am NOT wearing hearing aids. A metal hip, botched bunion operation and now hearing aids, no! I know he was only trying to help, but really.

How sad that sounds, get hearing aids because then they won't have to repeat themselves; and you know what? I get irritated with my mum, too, when she can't hear... I will try much harder now...

Chapter 26
Burnt-out Mummy

I woke up this morning not at all rested; I had been foolish enough last night to try on the dress I had planned to wear to my friend's wedding, after a very fun night spent with colleagues. Bloated with food and drink, I decided it is seriously not ok to wear. Thus started my night of what I suppose was a mental tour around various shops trying to find something to fit my body that feels large and distended. It's crazy, the wedding is this morning and I am going shopping... Not only that, I have just weighed my focused mind and body and discovered no change on the dreaded scales.

'Know who you are,' I hear as I start to slip down the slippery slope of condemnation.

'Yes,' I reply. 'I am a woman whose story starts with Genesis where we walked in communion with God. It does not start as a struggling drug addict, a failure, a promiscuous ex-model. It continues through the story of creation evolving and changing. It carries on where Jesus the rescuer comes and shows signs and wonders that point us back to God and ends with *His* victory; *His* victory as death becomes submissive and I am united in my relationship with God.'

I *will* remember this as I walk through this day. I *will* remember that I am an heir and so I am loved and blessed and cherished, and I will try to see myself in that light when the image I see reflected in the mirror does not match up with the perfect image that I would like. These are the words that God whispered to me via my phone as I pounded the cross trainer and listened to Rob Bell.

Yesterday I got out my old sewing machine and took in and up the dress that I eventually bought that day nearly a *year* ago!

Shall I tell you how it has been?

The celebrations and the pain, the tortuous route I still meander on.

I have found my life exhausting: working as a therapist with people who have been severely traumatised is a massive privilege and honour and I love it, but it does not leave much for those I love so much within my own family.

There have been so many family issues that are, I am sure, what so many of us face on our journey as parents, but I have really struggled with these ones of recent days. The kind that leave you feeling that you can't go on without being stained by a type of madness. Children bring so many joys and so many challenges, and our hopes and dreams for them sometimes lie in pieces on the roads we walk.

So how do we go forward, boldly or with trepidation, with our fingers stuck in our ears as we sing to drown out the sound of anything or always looking backwards in fear and continually falling over? I am at the place where the future is very uncertain and I am attempting to put down the pursuing sense that I have not done enough and the price being paid is too high. So I will tell you what I am going to do: I am going to take my faithful laptop to New Wine – yes, I am going to camp in England! Those of you who know me well will know that I am not a camper unless there is a proper bed and suitable weather, hot, and, of course, a well-stocked fridge!

Last time I camped in England was on my honeymoon, and as you know that was pretty disastrous; not a particularly good start for a marriage that has, in fact, this month survived 22 years! I cannot believe it – sometimes it has been survival and other times blessings and joy. Where has the journey gone? The children that I juggled as I ran a pre-school and trained as a counsellor are grown up or growing. I sound old, but I am not, and I am still eagerly, most of the time, unless I am exhausted, looking to the future.

So I am about to embark on another adventure – this time the tent is a nine-man tent. Three out of our four children are coming and I have a large double blow-up bed, which I hope will stay inflated and I will not be flung out by my husband turning over suddenly!

Tomorrow I will turn my laptop on and continue to tell you what has been happening and how God is talking to me. I can't wait...

***

New Wine (a sort of Spring Harvest but camping) and new wine skins; I don't want to burst after all!

Here I am in an environment of prayer and praise surrounded by people who love me. Why am I unable to receive anything?

Inside me there seems to be a very dangerous reservoir of tears that I thought I had released already and now I am afraid that if I go to its edge, I may not stop my howling.

I have arrived exhausted and stumble around seeking a safe place. Eventually we (I do have one trusted friend who I think can handle me in this condition; I am sure that all the others who are with me could too – I just don't give them the chance) find a sofa in the back of a healing prayer seminar. My heart is beating too fast; it needs to slow down.

The dam that has been threatening to burst overflows in the embrace of my friend and the awesome power of God settles, like a band of heat around my forehead, as I pour out my prayers for our children: prayers of protection for their minds and bodies. Sobs that have threatened me like an impending thunderstorm move like waves through my body and mingle with sounds of anguish that come from a place deep within me. Is this how we are made in God's image, when we experience pain that almost breaks us in half, as we consider those we love and the possibility of the pain they may experience in their lives because of choices they make?

Writing this last paragraph, I remember that I have already sobbed with someone so close to me, that she walks my pain with me, but maybe once is not enough, and maybe twice is not either! It says in Psalm 56:8 that God collects our tears in a bottle (New Living Translation). He must have many bottles of mine.

The trouble with these Christian events is that it is hard to not feel like a bit of a loser if you don't go to everything. I am sure this is a misconception, but there you go – probably something about missed opportunities – so here I sit in the loudest coffee shop imaginable, surrounded by people worshipping. I sit, the only one among thousands, with my laptop, drinking cappuccino and feeling ok. I sit at the back and try to be inconspicuous, but that is hard when you are the only one. I want to be here but not be overwhelmed by all the people. I am desperate to hear from God but it is hard to find a place of stillness and calm here.

Oh yes, by the way, I slept in my tent and my airbed did not go down and I did not get cold and my body did not ache too much! How amazing is that? And it's not raining.

Voices and faces are speaking across the venue; strange how a stranger's voice can speak into my life:

God is the colour of hope. There is so much pain in the world, but life is too short not to embrace it. Go for prayer when you first get here!

Now that is something I have been resisting, so maybe when my battery runs totally flat I will do that, and I will let you know what happens.

Being exhausted and unable to even sit there any longer, I left the venue to see if there was a chance I could find the same sofa as yesterday. The venue is empty, however, and I sit in the same place as the day before, but in a slightly different mood. I want to hear from God and I imagine that someone will come and minister to me, but no one comes. I am so tired, weariness is deep within my bones; my bones feel like they are leaking trauma – is that too big a word? No, and they are leaking it into my bloodstream. And before I know it I am asleep and there is a seminar going on. I am shocked at my exhaustion, and yet I feel quietly revived by God and His presence. I think I am now able to stop avoiding people and engage again with the human race.

Why do I do that? I assume that a moment of stillness must mean that I am fixed and can resume normal life. I do not allow myself the luxury of extended time, the luxury that I would not have the trouble allowing a client, but I realise as I write that I possibly don't allow my close family that either! Now that is a troubling thought! Anyway, it turned out to be not exactly true; I still kept my head down when I saw those I did not know well, but was able keep my promise to paint my friend's children's nails!

Now, as the sun goes down, I am at peace, as I sit in my tent alone, listening to the mix of distant worship of different venues filtering across the fields to me. Yes, God is worthy of our praise!

***

The recap; the beginning of the year finds me seeing my father after a time of seven months, post the 'Zimmer throwing' incident.

I had known it was ok with God if I didn't put myself in a position where the risk of emotional harm was possible from my dad, and so I had calmly kept my distance.

I had come across an old friend outside church on New Year's Eve who had asked about Dad. I had told him that I would go and see Dad if he asked me, as then I would know his intention. I hope *you* know that you should never say anything like that idly, as the obvious happens – you are challenged to do something!

Within two hours my sister had rung me to say that Dad had asked to see me, as he did not want to go into the New Year without making things right with me. So I went. It was strange because as I walked across the room to him, I realised that I was an adult and I had not even prepared myself as I usually did with my mantra of 'don't rise to the bait, ignore him when he is unkind, etc.' His first words were, however, 'You have to accept her.'

He was, of course, referring to his girlfriend. However, his apparent joy was plain to see, witnessed by the tears that streamed down his face and his outstretched hands. So we sat holding hands and talked of the children and my life with David. It was a special moment that was not to last for long, but it was there for that time nonetheless.

So my challenge for this year is: live intentionally, pray faithfully, be enthusiastic.

So where did that challenge go? What happened?

My intention was so good: revere my husband, be submissive, but hey, you can imagine how hard that was!

I seem to stumble around in my life sometimes and almost don't know which way is up. And the struggle to let my husband lead is as big as it has always been. I hope I am not the only one out there who struggles with this.

January continued with God telling me that He has blessed me already and I have forgotten: writing gifts, guitar, a room of my own to be in, as well as a husband and work and prosperity.

Prosperity, huh! David told me I couldn't have a holiday unless we went to New Wine where he would serve as a steward. I was so cross.

'I don't want that,' I shouted.

I refused to consider it. As you can see, submission is not a challenge that I can even remember.

Then a client I was working with spoke of the love of camping that her husband had given her and, in that moment, she spoke a blessing over me. And I realised that God was going to bless me as I agreed to go to New Wine.

***

It is very strange how burnout creeps up on people; or rather it did on me when I was not expecting it. Even with hindsight that in some way informs me of why I am in this position, I cannot pierce the fog that has enveloped my head and to some degree my heart.

To be so tired as to feel unable to even sit upright sums up how deep the exhaustion had become. There are some reasons that are obvious, and I think they reflect the changing role of women. If you, like me, work outside the home as well as in it, you will identify with this.

When situations arise, and I think the ones that come along like waves when you parent teenagers are particularly exhausting, you need to be firmly rooted or else you will be swept away by the torrent. Check out these journal entries of mine during the time of my son's final year in primary school, he is now 14 and I have still not learnt my lesson:

I have been suffering with terrible headaches for the last four days. I knew that it was due to stress but I couldn't work out why.

As September was fast approaching I have been feeling increasingly worried about my youngest child starting secondary school. He has not had an easy time of it and so I have been feeling concerned with how he is going to manage life in a whole new environment. You would think it would get easier with it being my fourth time, after all.

I have decided to do something very different for me and that is to say, 'NO.' I have cancelled helping in Alpha and have backed out of worship group. It might not sound much to you, but let me tell you that for me it is highly significant. It shows my vulnerability and I don't do that easily. People think I am ill if I stop doing everything. But I know that my anxiety has a good reason and its most likely cause is because I didn't seek God; I just accepted the invitation to serve. I thought, wow they want me to do that, how fab, I am valued, etc. I have charged off stroking my own ego and now am about to fall apart. Anyway I did it: I made the phone calls, wrote the emails and guess what? They were all lovely to me and my headaches went away immediately and have not returned!

**

Parenting smaller children is different in its stresses. Remember, these are my views and experiences. I would feel swamped in guilt when the pressure of work would mean that I sent my children to school when they were not 100% and the best thing for them would have been to be tucked up under a duvet in the front room. I would feel assuaged by thoughts of failure when I was too exhausted to play with them; I had run a pre-school for most of their younger days. I would feel guilt that we did not have enough money to do as much as others seemed to do. I would feel terrible when my anger towards one of them would result in a look of fear that I recognised from my childhood. I did not want to be like my father, after all!

The different ages bring out the same feelings, after all; I said I was working this out as I go along, a bit like parenting.

***

Here is an excerpt from my journal from when my son had just started secondary school:

He informs me on awakening Monday morning that he has a stomach ache. As all working mothers know, this is a time of guilt and uncertainty, same as when they are young. Shall I insist he goes to school or shall I take a day off and possibly fall into the trap of encouraging him to stay away, rather than face the task of making new friends? Honestly it is so hard to be a mum sometimes. Well, after a round of 'put your clothes on', 'no' and 'come on, ok I'll do it for you!' to re-entering his room and finding him back in his underwear and his uniform in the rubbish bin, we finally make it downstairs for breakfast. I am doing well now, encouraging and staying calm. I am full of suggestions and coping strategies. And he reluctantly leaves clutching the 40p sweet money for on the way home. I sigh with relief and prepare my breakfast when the doorbell goes and there he is. 'I can't do it. I can't walk down there.'
'Yes you can. What's the matter?'
'I don't know. I just can't do it.'
'Well, you have to. I will get in trouble with the police.'

You can tell that I am getting rather desperate now. So what can you do when your child refuses to go to school? You wrap your bowl of cereal in cling film and say you will drive them. So off we go, me clutching my bowl and work bag and we head to my car. Once out on the road I see a friend and ask if Lewis can go with her. He reluctantly goes with her and I start to feel a bit better. My husband turns up (this is unusual where coping with a crisis with the kids is concerned) and offers to go and speak to the school. To say I am relieved is an understatement.

I am only at work an hour when the school rings: he is in the sick room. Oh no, has he been sick? No, as it turns out. I am holding on tentatively to the memory of him lying on his stomach this morning, reading the *Beano*, very happy until I say, 'Come on get dressed,' and recalling his response of, 'Ow, my stomach, it hurts.' (Add to that memory a bent-over child who suddenly is unable to stand upright.)

Calls back and forth through the day result in me fluctuating between a mother who knows her son so well and a mother who needs consoling by her wise colleagues. The final phone call was one of those coded ones, where one person (me) asks all the questions and the other party just says yes or no:

'So is he still there?'

'Yes, we are just eating lunch together.' (There's a clue to how he is getting on in that statement.)

'Is he sitting there with you?'

'Yes.'

'Can I just ask you questions?'

'Yes.'

'So will you be cajoling him back to class?'

'Yes.'

'Do you think he is ok?'

'Yes.'

'Ok, thanks.'

I go home relieved and get ready for my client, but my son does not come home! It is only 3.30 pm but he left school an hour before. I have visions of him running away from his wicked mother. I am pretty sure he wouldn't do that, but not 100%. So I have to start work not knowing if he is ok. I feel terrible until my husband appears in the garden with him. I feel exhausted now, but there you go. I am just a 'normal' woman.

***

Do you ever get up in the morning and your head is immediately full of 'stuff'? Anything from what is happening to, in my case, how to manage the new puppy.

Did I tell you I am getting another dog? As if our large German Shepherd/Rottweiler-cross Cleo is not enough! David says once I get an idea in my head that there is no stopping me. Well that is not entirely true: God's word does, and this morning is no exception.

It's 7:00 am and I am in my room. I have come to pray and read but my thoughts are careering around my head like a herd of wildebeest. Then it happens: I see out of the corner of my eye a piece of glass that has the words of Psalm 55 printed on it: 'In the morning, O Lord, you hear my voice; in the morning I lay my requests before you and wait in expectation.' It stops me dead in my mind-careering tracks. To wait in expectation, that is what I need to do.

Life just gets in the way sometimes, though – children, work, homework, and thoughts of a new puppy arriving tomorrow.

I was in my room reading. In fact, I had just finished and I felt the prompt of God (through the Bible study notes writer, Jeff Lucas – honestly, sometimes he is so annoying) to continue what I had started and to share what I had discovered.

I like to do different things: read different books, find alternative ways to engage with God, and my newest discovery was Andy Flanagan's *God 360 Degrees*. So Andy and Jeff are my inspiration today.

Do you suffer from anger, rage, malice, slander and filthy language? This was what it was all about. I don't think I am as bad as I used to be, but on reflection and with God's gentle pointing I realise that sometimes I do resort to my old tactics. Yes it's true, sometimes I still totally lose it. Now I know it is not so often but I still do occasionally. It is a truth that is hard to face.

The other night there was a programme featuring Griff Rhys Jones; he was talking about anger. He was talking to friends about what he was like and he was mortified to find out that he had been, and was still, a very difficult person to live and work with.

Well, I suppose I am rather fearful of discovering that too. I reckon I am a bit of a pain at times, and I lose it over crazy things, like labels on coffee jars.

This morning the challenge is to write out the words: anger, rage, malice, slander and filthy language and to allow God to speak, to challenge. Well, He has and I have discovered.

It all stems from anger and my desire to get things done my way in my time.

Phew, there you go. It's out.

And now I have been instructed to burn the piece of paper and ask for forgiveness, and also to change my behaviour.

***

So how did I do?

I didn't have to wait long too long. I went into my house to find my son moaning.

'I feel sick.'

I immediately went into calm but efficient mummy mode.

'Come on you will be fine, I will give you some Calpol, and it's only a cold.'

After breakfast:

'I feel giddy.' Calm mummy mode is now starting to wobble a bit.

'You'll be fine.'

Inside I am thinking, 'Oh no, I hope I am right and it's not that bug that's going around.'

Every now and then I think back to my time with God and the burning of my anger...

We leave for school and work – my son, my daughter and her friend and me. My son is not too happy and I am trying to chivvy him along. Stopping along the road to his school I let him out of the car.

'No, I can't, I feel sick.'

'Come on now, you are fine.' My voice is now rising as my plans are being thwarted.

'Oh, get back in, I will drive you to the school gate.'

I am by now getting fed up. Didn't last long, did I?

Outside the school I now look like the classic cross mother: my son is trailing behind as I walk quickly into school.

'Come on, everyone will see you making a fuss.' I really can't believe that I am so stupid. Why can't I keep my mouth shut? My mouth is on a roll. Thankfully a teacher that I know is in the office and I can turn my son over to her and her calm demeanour. Thank goodness for her care.

I feel bad as I drive to work. I am fairly certain that I have done the right thing, but I am a counsellor as well as a mother, and I know that children who are not listened to suffer. Am I being one of those mothers?

As it turns out, I was right: he was ok, but I didn't handle the situation very well. God has a long wait for me to be the woman I want to be, let alone the one I am supposed to be.

So yesterday was me leaving aside anger and not doing too well. And today is putting on new garments of compassion, humility, gentleness, kindness and patience. Honestly, life is one long challenge sometimes.

So this is how it goes: once again a lesson learnt via my son.

I spent time with God and drew an image of myself writing the words that describe my garments, alongside the images.

Patience: next to my feet – my children are forever telling me to stay still when they talk to me.

Humility: written next to my head, as I know that it is an attitude of mind.

Gentleness and compassion: alongside each arm as they are able to hug or hurt.

And kindness: by my legs because I know that kids are unkind when they kick.

Once I had done my not-so-splendid piece of artwork, I really prayed, asking God to help me, as I knew that my son probably would not want to go to school and I needed patience and wisdom to deal with it.

What do you reckon? How long did I last?

Not long.

He is in bed.

'Mum, I feel ill. I feel dizzy.'

'Come on,' is my reply. 'I will give you some Calpol.' (What did we do before Calpol?)

'I'm ill, I'm ill,' the chant begins.

'You'll be ok. You don't have P.E.'

'Yes I do.'

Oops, not the right thing to say.

'Come on, I will help you.'

I *gently* and *patiently* help him with his shirt and tie and jumper.

'Come on, get up and put on your trousers.'

The chant continues.

'I'm ill, I'm ill.'

'Come on, don't keep saying that. I am going to get cross.'

My *patience* is fading fast.

'I'm ill, I'm ill.'

'Stop it. Get dressed.'

No *patience* or *gentleness* in sight now.

I can almost hear God telling me to calm down. I am not out of control but I am aware of being totally frustrated, and the lesson of half an hour earlier is echoing in my ears. I stop and am overwhelmed by compassion as I realise again that I want to do things my way. My son, on the other hand, has a stinking cold and two hours of P.E. and a new puppy arriving. What is it about being 11 that I have forgotten?

I wrap my arms around him and tell him to change into his own clothes.

Why was it so hard? Old habits die hard.

Chapter 27
Who am I?

My battle with anger still continues. As my daughter said to me just now in response to my comment of, 'A counsellor and issues with anger, sorry.'

'Yeah, it's a bit strange that you get angry and work with anger as a counsellor.'

Wow, children have a way of saying it how it is, and I feel shame. It's really pathetic that I just lose my temper, and all because I feel that life is unfair and I am tired and so I become defensive. It's no good. I need to try and deal with this! Does it happen to you? I hope I am not alone.

***

I feel guilt that my issues around my weight have caused my girls to look at themselves with critical eyes, and they are so beautiful both inside and out. I feel guilt that I am often too tired to have 'deep and meaningful conversations' at midnight and wish they would go to bed, then in a moment know that I should treasure and hold these times close to my heart as they will not last forever. I feel shame that I do not stay an adult when they challenge me and do that very annoying ganged-up mocking thing, forgetting to understand that they are working out who they are and that it is good that they laugh about me together.

I still feel bad sometimes when we don't have a lot of extra cash, but then I am quicker now to get a grip on myself and see what we do have.

So back to burnout: what is it and how do we stop it?

Well, one thing is to know that it is a natural occurrence when you juggle many things, and that it is important to listen to the wise counsel of sisters and friends who challenge you about taking on another thing. When you write in your journal that you are not what you do but that your identity is in Christ, that you actually pay attention to it and not be like me, reviewing my journal for my book seven months later to unearth the secrets behind burnout. If we have our identity in Christ we will not seek the approval of others, as we will intentionally walk in His will. But it is so hard, isn't it?

Should I continue to tell you about the present whilst looking back at the past?

Yes, I think I will, because hindsight is most useful when it is seated in the present.

***

I have come to France, or should I say we have? I know I said that David had said that we could only have one holiday, but then we were invited to use the holiday home of friends Eric and Jenny, who all those years ago gave us years of family holidays in their home on the south coast of England! What a surprise blessing, and not the only one; a friend of David's whom he worked with also invited us to Majorca for a week without the kids, with him and his girlfriend! We only had to pay the airfare, we both managed to take time off work at short notice and, hey presto, the obedient wife gets a blessing from her husband! Even that was a struggle – submitting to going, I mean, as I had never met his friends before, but we got on fine and had fun and once again I realised I was exhausted and needed the rest.

Here's a thought: do we spend most of our time being tired?

So what about 'identity in Christ' that I was talking about before?

Back to France. Even on holiday I can still feel responsible for the happiness levels of all my family, and my concern is often shown in a kind of control, as I think I know best.

We are staying in a lovely French house, with a terrace for the morning and a balcony, where I sit now, for the afternoon, and I still manage to feel outrage at being misunderstood.

I arise each day early and read and write and pray, mostly alone, but sometimes two of my daughters come and sit too. And then the men – my husband and son – eventually get up and it all changes. Well, it did yesterday anyway.

A quick question, 'Are you ok?' results in, 'Well, I would be if you didn't ask questions like that!'

And the tone for the rest of the day is set. A hormonal daughter, an offended mother and a cranky husband result in a day where it is true to say that my daughter and I cannot snap out of it.

If I went back to the time in New Wine, I would have to tell you that I had received a challenge about not living offended and that ever since, I had done exactly that. I can't say that it is worse than normal, but when something is highlighted by God, you cannot escape.

If my identity is in Christ, then why do I get offended? Is God always on my case or am I oversensitive? It must be the latter. So how do I beat this thing?

I did talk to David about it this morning and he said that I sound like I am nagging. In that very moment, after we had been out alone to buy croissants and it was all very lovely, I very nearly went into a sulk at the 'nagging' word, but pulled myself up short. I realise I am able to sulk – how awful is that; I hate sulking! Once again the word of God rings true: don't take the speck out of your brother's eye until you have taken the plank out of your own!

So who am I? And who are you?

Are you someone who cares but gets it wrong sometimes, or are you, as the voice of condemnation says, a failure because you can't make everything ok for everyone all the time?

I am going to believe the former, and then I hope my habit of sulking will diminish.

Back to the recap: January journal entry.

Psalm 23:

'The Lord is my shepherd, I lack nothing. He makes me lie down in green pastures, he leads me beside quiet waters, he refreshes my soul.'

I love that, don't you?

To be made to lie down is like being a little child, and the one who is looking after you knows best. I have heard it said, 'Sometimes the Lord calms the storm; sometimes He lets the storm rage and calms the child.'

How do we allow God to calm us despite our circumstances? Time with Him is definitely part of the answer.

'Putting down rage frees up love,' is another quote that resonated from a morning preach and still does today. A bit like putting down the urge to sulk – absolutely ridiculous!

This entry is followed by an incident with my father that I am not happy to put in here as it will affect how others think of him, but suffice it to say it tripped me up and I fell 'like Alice down the rabbit hole', as my journal says, and resulted in me becoming enraged again.

Being a Christian is so hard, isn't it?

There are so many twists and turns.

But I eventually sought prayer with someone and the Lord gave me Revelation 22:14:

Blessed are those who wash their robes, that they may have the right to the tree of life and may go through the gates into the city.

So once again I relinquish the rage that I so readily pick up in an effort to live free.

2 Corinthians 10:5 contains the answer:

We demolish arguments and every pretension that sets itself up against the knowledge of God, and we take captive every thought and make it obedient to Christ.

The Message Bible gives 2 Corinthians 10:3-6 this way:

The world is unprincipled. It's dog-eat-dog out there! The world doesn't fight fair. But we don't live or fight our battles that way – never have and never will. The tools of our trade aren't for marketing or manipulation, but they are for demolishing the entire massively corrupt culture. We use our powerful God-tools for smashing warped philosophies, tearing down barriers erected against the truth of God, fitting every loose thought and emotion and impulse into the structure of life shaped by Christ.

The question is, how do I get ahead of my thoughts that so readily convert into feelings?

Do we really have loose thoughts, emotions and impulses?

Absolutely!

That is one of the reasons that Cognitive Behavioural Therapy is such a buzzword in our culture today. We have discovered that our thought life affects our being, our physical health, in a very impacting way. So once again the Bible is ahead of its time!

At around this time someone gave me a Post-it note. It said: 'Tell Susie – Jesus released her from her relationship with her father long ago… He has no expectations of her!'

Wow, what a word!

Still… I keep picking up the burden.

Why?

Whispers of doubt, not being made to conform to God's will and also the ability, I suddenly realise, to listen to Satan instead of God!

God lavishes us with good things and we push Him away without even meaning to; we are so used to the condemning voice.

Here's a funny thing – well, it made me smile anyway – my phone just buzzed here in the south of France. It was someone asking to see me for couples counselling. I suggested that I could give them someone else's name as I am away, but they said they would wait, as I come highly recommended!

Come on, that is funny. After all, I have just told you about my marriage!

Just discovered a journal entry that says, 'Just realised that my children and husband may one day read my journal and I want you all to know how blessed I am to be your mother. I love you so much; my heart bursts to have such amazing children and husband.'

Now before I continue, I want you to know that I journal from the standpoint of a place of love. I couldn't be this honest if that was not true.

The struggle continues nonetheless.

Chapter 28
God speaks

A quiet morning finds me in a garden at the foot of a huge oak tree. I sit and wait for the Lord to speak.

This is the dialogue between the Lord and me in my head.

'The birds sing, so many. How do you hear them all?' I ask. And I wait.

'Come on my soul, come on my soul, let down the walls, and sing my soul.' I sing this recently learnt song in my spirit.

I look up at the tree and my focus is drawn to the many vines and creepers that cling to it, and my conversation in my spirit with God starts in earnest.

'Even though they cling like vines, my hold is deeper, wider and stronger.'

'Your roots go deep: do not be distracted by the clamouring, by the calls of anguish.'

'Know your roots and me. I will nourish you.'

'I will be your sustenance; even in the drought your roots can reach moisture.'

'Why does the clamouring go so high?' I ask.

'Because I am strong enough.'

'Sometimes I feel overwhelmed,' I say.

'I know.'

'How can I manage?' I mumble.

'See the Canada geese? They fly in formation; they follow their leader. They take turns at the front. Don't be afraid to fly behind the leader. See what happens when one goes off on its own.'

'Panic,' I answer as I watch one flounder as they fly past.

'Sending out roots requires determination; doing the journey to get there, making the effort, choosing to take up the offer. Be nurtured, as you nurture.'

So you see, all you mothers, daughters, sisters, and men, of course, the bottom line is that we who nurture must ourselves be nurtured.

***

I visit my dad with Millie and I am anxious as we arrive as he has not let up in his continued harshness. When we arrive there is a big guy covered in tattoos sitting on my father's bed talking to him; he is accompanied by his young Thai wife. As we stand in the doorway, my father introduces me as his bad daughter. I once again feel the pain of his rejection. I try to justify myself by saying that I have brought Millie to see him, before she goes back to university. He immediately minimises that, saying she wanted to come; he has no idea that it was my suggestion. Then the tattooed man speaks up:

'Do you know what is says in Genesis, Dennis? God made everything good, including your daughter.'

In a moment I am aware that this stranger is protecting me from my father and his unkind words.

God was ahead of me once again.

A few weeks later finds my sister and me in A&E all night with Dad, who shouts at us when we arrive but, over the course of the night, gradually accepts our care. His girlfriend is away and therefore we are able to access him.

At church the same day, only hours later, my friend Adam preaches and the Lord speaks through Hebrews 12, again.

Adam's message went something like this, according to my journal:

'There is a cast of thousands; it's not about me. It's all about God, His plan, His way.'

I need to get over myself.

Where fears are stilled and strivings cease. That is where I will find you.

What will you say when I am stilled?

Does my faith become challenges and problems to solve?

Do I try to do good because God loved and forgave me?

Or do I think I need to do good in order to stay right with God and earn value in my own sight?

When fears like the breeze stop, then you feel the heat of the sun.

When I put down fear, then I am free to be me. When I cease to strive, then I am able to receive God's blessing.

Striving limits abundance, so why do I strive? Do I not trust?

Yet when I let go, I receive God's blessing.

***

Majorca with David. I receive a call that Dad is ill again and may die. I go to the empty beach in the early hours, alone, and sit at a hotel table before it opens for custom.

The early morning light settles peace on me like a blanket.

Prayers and pleading come silently from within me as I watch the sun change the colours of the sea.

A Spanish morning greeting brings tears, unbidden, to my eyes and silent words:

'Dad, don't die.'

Coffee and tears: he taught me to love these things, and also to hate.

But thoughts of death only bring to the surface the good things of the past.

The waters lap. Dad did not die.

So even on holiday I am pursued by my dad!

***

27th May: Dad may die.

Andrew, my brother, comes over from America to see Dad, as they think he may die, and then Uncle Ron dies.

Does it seem like that to you? Trouble comes like the number 9 bus, in groups?

Poor Mum – her husband is ill and could die and she cannot see him as they are estranged, and then her last surviving sibling dies.

All a bit too much, but God knows, and as she receives the call from Spain regarding her brother, Andrew, my brother, is standing beside her in the kitchen. She would not have wanted anyone else to be with her at that time!

In the midst of trouble we find you, Lord.

I am alone with Dad in hospital. His girlfriend is due back today. I have stayed in England to provide protection as he seems better, when he is not obsessing over her. Mandy is in Spain with Mum for the funeral of Uncle Ron, Andrew has gone home to America and I am sitting with my dad about to play Scrabble. He doesn't really want to but has reluctantly agreed.

'To give me the pleasure of beating you,' I laugh.

We munch strawberries together and I reach for the board and *she* arrives.

In a moment, she is all that exists and I sit there simmering. He wants me to share his pleasure but I cannot. This relationship is responsible for a lot of the pain of the last decade.

Days of pain and accusation follow and he chooses her again and again over me and my children, and I am like the inimitable Rottweiler where my children are concerned, so I walk away... again.

***

6th June.

My journal is a constant run of things that have been spoken in church and alone with God. This day finds us looking at a difficult passage – Romans 3:10–18.

As it is written:
'There is no one righteous, not even one; there is no one who understands; there is no one who seeks God.
All have turned away, they have together become worthless; there is no one who does good, not even one.'
'Their throats are open graves; their tongues practise deceit.'
'The poison of vipers is on their lips.'
'Their mouths are full of cursing and bitterness.'
'Their feet are swift to shed blood; ruin and misery mark their ways, and the way of peace they do not know.'
'There is no fear of God before their eyes.'

Pretty harsh stuff, eh?
Are you like me? When the passage is hard or I have arrived tired or I get bored by the heaviness of it all, my mind wanders and I end up with scraps or gems that I prefer to look at!
Here are my scraps and gems:

No scheme of man can pluck me from His hand! Focus on God, not on your dad! Don't give it any more airtime. Be careful how you think and act. We are made to worship God. Our mouths paralyse others. Our mouths criticise others. Our mouths wound others. Our mouths damage others because we discount our sin.

Now that was more than a scrap!
How do we do this Christian walk then? With difficulty!
Striving:

It's almost that striving is my default position, the one I relate to the most. How do I stop that, how do you stop that?

I read in a magazine recently that because we are so stressed these days, we need more holidays; one a year is not enough.

***

6.00 am:
From deeply asleep I am woken, the dialogue goes like this:
'Susie.'
'Yes.'
'Come and be with me.'
'Really, is it you?'
'Yes it is.'
So I am here for the first time in ages, weary, aware of God's interventions that have saved us from disaster (I can't say what has happened but, suffice it to say, He saved us from a calamity) and we are being offered a second chance.

God is calling me, He wants me to be equipped and ready, and I feel like I am standing with my arms outstretched and God is putting my armour on me, like I am a child being dressed by a parent.

I remember a dream from the previous night, where I am trying to do more work in the night, as I am full in the day, and suddenly the realisation is that I am trying too hard, even as I sleep, and the words 'the battle belongs to the Lord' ring in my mind.

My reading that day is John 21:1–25.

So I read with an enquiring mind, wondering what He is going to say today.

They go out and catch nothing; Jesus appears and tells them to fish on the other side. Peter realises it is Jesus when their nets burst, but only after John points it out and then Peter immediately jumps in and swims to Jesus.

Do you relate to someone in the Bible? I do. One is Peter, for his charging-about way of doing things. The other is Mary Magdalene because of her previous life.

The conversation that follows, when Jesus asks Peter how much he loves Him, has started to mean more to me recently because I am questioning just how much I love Jesus. Don't get me wrong – I do, but how much?

Peter also asks Jesus about John and he is told to not look at others so much, but at Jesus instead.

'I am so sorry, Lord; I have missed our early morning chats,' I confess.

'I am holding on to your hand. Don't be afraid,' He says.

'I am so grateful for the rats; they focused my mind to pray.'

What was meant as a plague to distress was turned into a blessing.

I was being refocused and clinging to my Father. When I heard His prompt, disaster was averted.

We had had rats in our ceilings and walls, and they were freaking me out to say the least. We had tried all the normal routes to get rid of them, but they were canny little critters. These rodents, like I said, brought me to a place of pleading with God, and so I was focused on Him and thus able to hear His quiet whisper, so a very serious situation was averted!

Pray for your children; the enemy is like a hungry lion that waits to destroy.

***

In our church, we have quiet mornings every now and then, led by wonderful spiritual people. They are delicious. I urge you to allow yourself time to go if they are available in yours. This is what happened in July. More notes:

All clamours.

Look at me, listen to me, argue with me, be hurt by me.
And the Lord beckons, an invitation.
Let go, and I do.
And in the stillness, alone with you, I find you, and
permission for a blessing.

I sat in the conservatory with the others in the morning sun, considering my surroundings and saw in the distance what I thought was a fig tree against a wall. We were instructed to find a place to be alone with God, once we had prayed and been given a verse to meditate on. The sight of the tree had set my heart racing as I considered a kind of biblical perspective on the day.

The verse given to us was Psalm 27:5:

For in the day of trouble he will keep me safe in his dwelling; he will hide me in the shelter of his sacred tent and set me high upon a rock.

So to my joy, I find it is a fig tree against a wall, and I sit at its feet and start to listen and talk with God.

My prayer and thoughts go something like this:

The battle belongs to the Lord. My role is to be someone who lets go. In trouble, let go. He will keep me safe in His dwelling. He will hide me in His tabernacle. He will set me on a rock.

Dialogue with God.

'So, if I let go will you do it?' I ask.

'Yes,' the answer.

'How?' I respond.

'You are letting go.'

'I know, but I struggle with not knowing.'

'I know. Look at the fig tree, what do you see?'

So I look and see a set of strong branches – they cling along a tall, strong wall. They are held in place by the wires that the gardener has placed there. The leaves are all green and there is fruit. The wall faces the morning sun and it grows in rich soil.

'So what have you learnt?'

'The health of the fig tree is dependent on certain things.'

'Good soil, good pruning, good wires to hold it in place and a good place to grow.'

As I sit there in the silence, the sweet music of blue tits chases away the moan of distant traffic. And I am soothed and God's arms enfold me.

'I am the gardener, I do the work, I show you the way you need to grow.

'I put supports in place, I cut off dead leaves and I enable good fruit to grow,' He says.

'You are the father who lifts me up away from the waves that threaten to overwhelm me. Sometimes I put up my arms; sometimes I am too afraid,' I whisper.

'When are you afraid?' He asks.

'When it all feels too big,' I reply.

'Why do you try and hold it then?' He asks.

'Because I have always done that. If I put it down, bad things may happen.'

'Ah,' He says.

I am surprised at his, 'Ah,' the next question, and my answer.

'What bad things?'

'I don't know.'

I asked my friend Dilys to pray with me.

'Break the ties that bind you,' I hear Him say.

I start to tell her that I feel like my hands are tied behind my back.

And we wait again.

Disappointment and discouragement overwhelm me.

And I feel so ashamed.

They are so insignificant (my thoughts).

I am ashamed to say them out loud.

But I do.

Then God reveals His truth in it all:

I have put my hands behind my *own* back.

No one put them there.

I don't need to.

I am not the sacrificial lamb.

I am not the scapegoat.

I suddenly realise my arrogance.

I have put myself in the place of God.

So I confess before my friend:

'Jesus was the scapegoat.

I am so sorry for my arrogance.

I tried to stand in your place, Lord, to take the shame and guilt.

And you had already taken it.

Sorry, Lord.'

Dilys then prayed for me and I knew I had to cover my hands in soil.

As she collected a jug of water, I started to cover my hands but could not stop and covered my arms as well.

She returned, poured out the water, and now I am clean.

I have shared a very intimate time with you, for one reason only – in the hope that it will encourage you. I have in no way got it sussed, but sometimes I find it helpful to hear how others do this thing called faith. Sometimes we need to do something symbolic in order to be obedient to God and for what He is saying to us to 'take on legs', so to speak

A quick interject:

On the terrace in France, reading John 21 and Jeff Lucas, I realise that God is causing me to reflect on what happened, again, on that quiet day. Jeff writes about how hard it must have been for Peter to be asked three times by Jesus whether he loved Him, but then goes on to say that, in the end, Peter says that Jesus knows all things. The heart is a deceitful thing and can trick us, as it had done me before, but to know that even Jeremiah realised that is an encouragement. Listen to this:

Jeremiah 17:9-10 in *The Message* Bible says:

The heart is hopelessly dark and deceitful, a puzzle that no one can figure out. But I, God, search the heart and examine the mind. I get to the heart of the human. I get to the root of things. I treat them as they really are, not as they pretend to be.

***

6.30 am

I sit, play guitar – badly – and write... it's not complicated.

My reading is Romans 5:3–5:

'Suffering leads to perseverance, perseverance leads to character, character leads to hope' (my paraphrase).

In *The Message* Bible it says it like this:

We continue to shout our praise even when we're hemmed in with troubles, because we know how troubles can develop passionate patience in us, and how that patience in turn forges the tempered steel of virtue, keeping us alert for whatever God will do next. In alert expectancy such as this, we're never left feeling shortchanged. Quite the contrary – we can't round up enough containers to hold everything God so generously pours into our lives through the Holy Spirit.

Isn't that fantastic? We never lose out with God!

So that morning, I start to pray for my dad... again.

Do you ever have times when you are praying for the wrong in someone else? Pointing a finger at them metaphorically speaking and finding three fingers pointing back at you? Well this was one of those occasions.

'Lord, may he know you.'

'Maybe he does already.'
'But why does he do that stuff?'
'Is he any different from you?'
'What about her?'
'Leave her to me.'

Chapter 29
Refiner's fire

17th July

I am plagued by an image that pursues my mind, taking up valuable space that could be free for blessing. I cry out:

'I want to be free of that image, Lord.

Please blot it out.

I love him.'

'I love him more!'

'I claim what was meant for harm for your glory Lord. I am going through the fire. May I be purified in this process, I turn my eyes to you, I cling to you, I hope in you.'

***

Life as a woman of God is full of the many twists and turns that life brings to us all. It is a constant struggle to focus on God. Sometimes I even wonder if it would be easier to not be a Christian. Am I too reflective because I am a woman of faith? But then, I cannot imagine being another way, because who would I turn to when it all hits the fan, as it does so often? How would 1 stay sane, even? David says that I see God everywhere and he is right; on a good day I do. I want to, and if I am focused, which I am often not, then I am aware of His presence. And I love it. It is crazy that I would even consider not focusing on Him, but we have to live and get on with life, don't we?

The other day I was reading John 21:6: 'He said, "Throw your net on the right side of the boat and you will find some."'

I was aware of the similarity of life now and then. They were unaware, the fishermen, that just on the other side of the boat was a huge catch just waiting for them. How often in life do we live unaware of God's blessing just around the corner?

***

At New Wine, I decided to go to an early morning meeting. Here is what happened (just to remind you, I had come away expecting a blessing from God and thus far am rather distressed at my burnt-out self):

'I sense someone here who comes with unexpectancy, and God has a bucket, full of the oil of joy, to pour over you,' the leader prophesies over us all.

'That's me,' I thought. 'I want that.'

Eagerly I sat and listened to the message. Here are some thoughts from it:

Don't run from refining fire, lean into the impossibility, He will be in there.

Joy will be in it, God is closer to you there than you can imagine.

Daniel 3:25: 'Look! I see four men walking around in the fire, unbound and unharmed, and the fourth looks like a son of the gods.'

God was there as they stood their ground.

Do you have ground you need to stand on? I do – worries for my son and my daughter will not be given to the enemy. The joy of the Lord is my strength.

When I listen to preachers I do it through my own circumstances, and even as I read my Bible it will depend on what is happening in my life as to what I receive from it. I suppose that is the same with everyone. I am aware as I reread my journal where my head was that day, how desperate I was, how troubled.

His kindness leads us into dependency. The refiner's fire brings joy; God's kindness takes away independency, self-sufficiency.

You can see what is being pointed out to me: the need to put down control, to become pure in my faith. Such a challenge.

Malachi 3:2 says:

But who can endure the day of his coming? Who can stand when he appears? He will be like a refiner's fire or a launderer's soap.

There are no alloys in the kingdom of God, no mixed metals. Pure gold will come.

When God is doing something in the fire, we must not run, but that's so hard, isn't it?

The preacher then went on to say this:

'The refiner's fire is God's greatest gift to you when you need to be stopped in your tracks!'

Don't you think that sounds crazy, but my experience cries out that it is the truth nonetheless. The trouble with me is that when the pressure is on rage comes out, but I must find the gold that is in the fire!

The preacher says this:

The only way to do it is to run towards the fire, not away from it. Don't listen to the enemy, who whispers that God has abandoned you. Know that the fire always leads to a blessing and enriches you as it brings more of Jesus.

At the end of the meeting, as is often the way, there was an invitation to come to the front, to stand before God and to confess when you have done things your own way. I, of course, went. Now remember, I don't trust people I don't know to pray for me, and so the invitation to everyone not at the front to be prayer pastors and to come and lay hands on us caused a ripple of concern in me. Anyway, this is what happened: I felt a hand on my shoulder and turned to look: it was a man. Now the general rules are girls with girls and men with men, when praying.

So I took a deep breath and thought, ok, so he is my witness, and continued, and then he put a hand on my other shoulder. I was then struggling to stay focused, but I managed it. When I turned, he put his arms around me and embraced me. After the hug, I turned to the front, now struggling to stay focused on God, and as I did he slid his hand up my neck, under my hair, and started to lightly massage me. It was at this point I walked away.

Now let me get something clear here. I am a hugger of both men and women, although in recent days I have been challenged about this because of a situation that had occurred with someone else. Christians are not immune to temptation!

Ok, you could well think that I am making a fuss about nothing, but with my history it felt like an all-out attack from the enemy. I did not let him totally sabotage my time with God, but it distracted me for the rest of the day, until I went for prayer with a friend. I was then assured that it was not me and that it was absolutely inappropriate. At this point I do want to say that New Wine put in place measures to ensure that men pray with men and women with women.

To ponder:

Do you think the enemy oversteps the mark all the time? It felt like it that day: I went for a blessing and he tried to wreck it. In the end he did not manage it, though, and I found God in the refining fire. In fact, I found amazing blessing; some of it came from those I was with who loved me, some came via my friend who prayed for me, and some came from an adopted little girl who physically struggled with groans of pain as she let go of her birth parents and trusted God with them. I have never seen someone so open to what God wanted and so open to showing the painful process at the same time. It truly blessed me as she allowed me to come within reach of her pain. And it taught me too.

The next early morning session: I went, determined not to be put off by the previous day.

'I am hungry for you Lord,' were the thoughts in my head, 'I want the fire.' I walked with a determination to the meeting and sat with two friends for safety. I did not even look for the man.

These are the notes I made on that session:

These are the enemy of the Holy Spirit:

Striving, using your own power leads to burnout and anger!

Press in to God, rest; it's peaceful, not full of anxiety.

The hairs on the back of my neck stood up as I listened to him. Oh dear, I do that all the time. No wonder I have no peace. How can I stop being me, is it something that is possible to put down?

The next enemy is form and structure: we lose power when we try to work everything out, when we use our natural wisdom. I am great at saying that God gave us intelligence and we need to use it. Even in my sleep, sometimes I wake with a plan hatching in my head, a solution to a problem.

I turn out to be not so smart, after all.

Another enemy is substitution; we put something else in God's place. Busyness is what I do; if I only work hard enough, if I put enough hours in…

Take a nap, or raise the dead: the reward is the same.

Don't you think that is strange – we can't earn His love, no matter what we do? Stop working so hard. Remember, these are my notes to me, and they are speaking loud and clear.

It's not the hours you put in that makes the difference; it's Jesus.

And here is a killer blow: good intentions do not make a difference; Jesus does. How often have my good intentions fallen by the wayside? I have lost count.

The invitation of the morning is to put down pursuit of a lifestyle and relinquish control to God. I had known in the back of my mind that I needed to publicly get on my knees before God and now was the opportunity. So I found myself undone before God, on my knees, sobbing, as I surrendered everything before Him: my life, my husband, my children, my family, my friends, my work, my very days.

At this point, I need to tell you that someone else laid hands on me: this time, a lady.

God spoke into my spirit and told me to lift up my arms, so I did. Then gently, ever so gently He metaphorically pulled what felt like a polo-neck jumper off my body – I felt it move over me, and eventually over my neck and face and I felt free to fully inhale. It was a jumper of anxiety, He told me, anxiety for others. All that was left was me, whom He loved.

That might sound strange or even weird to you; it is the risk you take when you are open – people can think you are crazy, but the thing is, it made total sense. I had not seen myself as anxious, but I so clearly was.

As I sat there at the front, there were only a few of us left; a couple of friends were talking together and there was a young woman kneeling near me. I started to say to her, as we smiled at each other, that God loved her, but could only get out the words, 'He loves *us*.' We cried together, safe in the knowledge. She asked me if I knew the *Narnia* story about Eustace, who had the dragon scales taken off him by God. In that moment, I heard the confirmation of what had just happened to me, when He removed the 'jumper'! I was free! The only problem would be if I tried to squeeze into the jumper again. And as you probably know already, it would not be long.

Still, now the jumper was off, I was able to put on the cape of blessing and pick up the cup of joy that my friend had seen for me yesterday. My prayer is that you too, will grasp the cup of joy.

Cup of joy
It's mine
Put down striving
It's mine
Let God be in control
It's mine
As I humbly submit
It's mine
As I put aside pride
It's mine
As I press in
It's mine
As I wait.

Do not be anxious about anything, but in every situation, by prayer and petition, present your requests to God.
Philippians 4 :6

I checked out my concerns with God like this:
'So what about work, Lord?'
'If you don't live anxiously, it will feel different. If you are consumed with fear about your family, you will struggle. Hold them lightly in your hands and let me do my work. Do not hinder me!'
I realise that my anxiety contaminates and hinders, and this puts it firmly in the arena of necessity to change.

As I felt better, I went to a few different seminars. One was on prophesy; it has always been my desire to be prophetic, and years ago I really sought God for the gift, but my work ethic and life had got in the way.

This is how I used to live, when my children were younger and I walked them to school: I would ask God for a word for someone or ask Him who I should talk to. One day I heard about a tragedy where a dad had died rescuing his children from a lilo; I did not know who the family were but they were on my mind.

Walking one day, I saw a mum with four young children and had the sense that they were the family. I asked God to put them directly outside my front door as I opened it, if He wanted me to talk to them. The next morning they were there. Thus started a relationship where I would go round to their house and spend time with them. Eventually I lost contact with them, then about a year ago I spied the mum in town and her name escaped my memory.

I ran out of the store hot on her heels, and she turned.

'Oh Sue, you will never know what you did for us. Thank you so much.'

I was shocked. I really did not do much; I was a friend to her and her kids but nothing much, I promise. Well, in my eyes anyway. She, on the other hand, did not think it was nothing and had experienced God's love via the meagre offering of a mum on the way to school.

Off I go to a teaching on prophesy, with her on my mind and a hunger again to be instrumental for God. This is what I learnt: 'Follow the way of love and eagerly desire gifts of the Spirit, especially prophecy' (1 Corinthians 14:1).

In the book of Revelation it says that we the redeemed will reign – we were created to be responsible for the outworking of God on earth. We are ambassadors – we need good communication.

Revelation 19:10 says that the witness of Jesus is the spirit of prophesy.

I want that gift.

In *The Message*, 1 Corinthians 14:3 says:

But when you proclaim his truth in everyday speech, you're letting *others* in on the truth so that they can grow and be strong and experience his presence with you.

See – it's the kindness of God that leads to repentance!

A few years ago God gave me the gift to pray for healing. I remember being the one called upon on a plane to Ukraine to pray for a painful stomach for one of the young people on the trip; I recall being surprised that they had asked me, but she did get better. I also always used to pray for my children when they were poorly, laying hands on them. Why have I stopped?

This is what I was left with after the seminar:

Remember your healing hands.

Ask God the questions we need to ask.

Ask God to see with His eyes.

Follow the way of love.

Prophecy is wrapped in grace.

Show people there is a God.

This living God knows all about them.

It is possible to have a living relationship with an invisible God and to speak into someone else's life.

Do you want these things?

Ask God for the required gifts; He loves to bless His children.

Chapter 30
She could have died

Days on, still in a head whirl.

When I write I often debate on whether it is useful to bring up so many of my struggles, but then again if I am not real you may think that it is all plain sailing, and it is not. It is, however, a choice too, as I am so good at saying to others...

This week brings my eldest daughter moving out into a flat and our relationship being on a much more equal, adult basis. It is also the week where I fight for my youngest child to have an education where they believe in him still, even though he has given up on himself. Tomorrow I will find out if I can get him into a new school, which is what he wants, but the wait is killing me! I am awake with hurting hips and shoulders. I am trying to put my worries down and when I read my Bible, like I did yesterday, the level of stress lifts for a while.

I knew when I saw the verses Ephesians 6:10–20 that it was all about putting on the armour of God, but it spoke to me so clearly again.

In *The Message* it says:

> Be prepared. You're up against far more than you can handle on your own ... Truth, righteousness, peace, faith, and salvation are more than words. Learn how to apply them.

I reckon it is a lifetime's work learning how to apply them; I keep picking up the stress, even though I do know absolutely that God is in charge. And then I feel ridiculous, when I think about women in Somalia, for example, having to make choices about which child to leave behind because they cannot carry them any further! I feel pathetic, but then I am like any mother – I want the best for my child, just like you.

So the risk for today is that I don't grasp what could be the last day of summer – the sun is actually shining – and spend it anxiously awaiting my meeting with the headmaster tomorrow. So I am going to walk on the beach with my dogs and have even planned to arrive as the tide goes out.

***

Three weeks on.

So many things have happened; all of them are unique to me in many ways and yet they are common to us all. My eldest daughter has left home, my next daughter has gone away to university to start a new course, my son has moved schools. So that means that yes, he did get into the school, and my youngest daughter fell onto the live rail at a station and was electrocuted! She is alive though she has suffered burns to her hips, but it is now a week on and she is getting slowly better, as am I.

It is 5.30 am and I have been awake for the past hour. I finally give in and go downstairs to write. The reason I am awake is Hollie: I woke with her in my mind, thinking about her and her life, her place in the family, her identity, who she wants to be, and the fact that she hasn't a clue.

I am thinking about how she grew up, what it is like to be the youngest daughter, carving a niche in a family who all have strong characters. I am wondering what it is like to be the youngest girl, but not to be the youngest, as her brother arrived after her. How does she make her mark? I awoke with an urge to write to her and about her so that she would know how I feel, how I love her and how I would die for her. I know it all sounds so 'dramatic', as David would say, but that is how I feel.

I walked into the A&E department a week ago and saw her lying there, glassy-eyed and crying with the remains of heart monitor wires – you know, those sticky patches that hold the wires still in place. Her skinny black jeans were folded down on one hip, revealing a deep blackened hole the size of a ten pence piece, and other burns which were less major, in the same area. Her shoulder and arms carried the bruises and dirt and grazes of a fall off a station platform. Her face, blackened by tears and a bleary intoxicated awareness that she had escaped death, just smiled and cried back at me.

As I met her eyes, I felt a wail rise from deep within me, a howl of pain and the awareness of her close escape, followed by a vision of how it could have been, with her lying still and white on a mortuary slab. Something changed and broke and was revived in me all at the same time.

In many ways, the details of the week don't matter here; you probably don't need to know the tug all of us mothers feel spoken about here, like the fact that the planned celebration Chinese meal for Millie, going off to start her new course, took place inside the burns unit. You also don't need to know that I had to decide whether I should go to Oxford as planned with Millie or whether I should stay with Hollie. It all sounds so trivial now. But at the time I wanted to do what was best for both of them. You don't need to know that Hollie and I have spent the past week lying on sofas, watching the 12 films we have hired and eating junk. You don't need to know that on day five my body went into shutdown, hurting in every muscle and bone, so bad that no painkillers touched it and that I felt and looked so old and fragile that I wondered how I ever managed to work at all.

As I write this now, I am aware that the fog has lifted and that I can indeed work. In fact, I saw a client yesterday. It all sounds so extreme, but those are the facts and the true feelings. I persuaded Hollie to walk gently through the woods with me and the dogs yesterday, to get her circulation going and to get some air. As I looked at the back of my angry daughter, who professed as we walked that the accident had not changed her, I thanked God for her angry back walking in front of me. And when I awoke at 4.00 am this morning, with her on my mind, I was glad that I could get up in the dark to write a letter to my daughter who did not die. That is what I am going to do now, but that is for her eyes only.

***

Well, life goes on, joy after joy and crisis after crisis, too. I have left my old job and now work only privately, which releases some time for me. But you know how it goes, it gets filled with something else; good things, but now I don't feel like there is a hand behind my back pushing me relentlessly forward.

7.30 pm and I am looking at a verse that is being spoken about on Sunday, when I am leading worship:

> With all this going for us, my dear, dear friends, stand your ground. And don't hold back. Throw yourselves into the work of the Master, confident that nothing you do for him is a waste of time.
> *1 Corinthians 15:58 (The Message)*

Don't you just love that verse? It says that we can be confident, that the work the Master gives us will be right for us and that we can throw ourselves into it.

So now for the original reason for the book: shame! Overwhelming, heart-stopping shame. As I got to work one day, a well-meaning friend told me with excitement written all over her face that she had found me on the internet. Topless pictures! At first I was almost pleased, until I looked and saw them. I was totally covered in shame. I went on to tell a couple of other friends, who also looked, along with their husbands! I hasten to add, it was no one's fault apart from my own. I had chosen to take my clothes off, but I was inconsolable; I felt violated, devastated and filthy. Any man could look at me; it was terrible.

This is what my journal says of that time:

24 3 08

Hollie was baptised yesterday – wow, how fantastic – she was brilliant – and God who knows her and loves her and blesses her. But Satan prowled and caught me unaware, unprotected. His talons caught my skin and tore me; shame enveloped me. Images on the internet seen by a friend launched in my mind a torrent of shame and tears. I was broken hearted. I looked like a child and grown men could look upon my body.

The next day I read about the Samaritan woman; she said that He (Jesus) told her everything she ever did. So I decided to turn it around. I can see how far I have come. I know what it is to be covered in shame and I pray that God will use me to help others. My battle is not against flesh and blood but against principalities and powers!

My journal reads:

I am rubbish: wounded.
I go to the Big Top and praising God lifts me out of my despair.
At the cross I bow the knee, where your blood was shed for me.
There's no greater love.
I know you love me.

It is sometimes as we are brought low that God stills us enough for us to experience His love.

I discovered a vital lesson that day. Worship silences the voice of the enemy. He cannot compete with our hearts being full of praise; we have the mind of Christ.

As a therapist, I know that people who struggle with anxiety use a huge amount of energy trying to live. Now I knew that I had lived my life always striving to do better, a driven woman trying to earn her stripes. I was trying to outrun my sense of not being up to scratch, and that was exhausting.

Chapter 31
Dormant blessings

Today.

The day was full of activity. My lovely friend Sarah came and spent a beautiful Saturday indoors, helping me organise my writing space, kitchen and under-stairs cupboard. What a star! Everyone needs a Sarah in their life!

It's funny how cleaning out can be a spiritual exercise. It felt today as if the removal of old things, unused and redundant, and the moving of useful things, like my writing desk to my daughter's bedroom to support her, and the giving of my husband's old computer corner to me, enabled our house to expand once again, and I experienced God's provision in what we already had but had not realised.

God often reveals things that have lain dormant for a season; suddenly they appear as if they are new, but really they have just been camouflaged while other activity takes place, or else they are waiting for the right time or prompt to appear. A bit like the writing thing for me: I always loved to write, but only as I allowed myself space to breathe, to remember, did the full urge surface.

Now I sit at my corner writing space, with everything in its place, and I feel calm and serene like the space. We have lunched and received a cry for help from Annie, the old lady over the road, whose urine bag had broken. We have changed it, dressed her and cleaned the toilet.

And we have pondered over the issues women like us face, with young beautiful daughters and changing bodies, and faces that betray the passing of time, and the often, retreating urge to maintain a healthy weight (in my case!). Why is it that so many women have issues about how they look?

I have had many conversations with women of various ages that have had a meltdown because the sun has come out and suddenly the body does not fit the summer clothes that have been retrieved from the back of the wardrobe.

So back to the garden, and Sarah and I are discussing how annoying it is that our sense of self is so often based on what we look like; we are still no nearer to a solution. We have swapped clothes, laughed and cried together, sat in awe at God's love for us and still we have issues and know that something minute can trip us off into a childlike tirade.

I am glad I am not alone in this, but still, I would like to be different. Truly, I don't think that rearranging the house will do that, but there will be fewer distractions to trip me up.

What did you leave behind when you became a new creation? A lifestyle? A mindset? A sense of fear? The thing is, when we become a new creation, our spirit is made new but our body, our mind, our very flesh, is still in a battle. These are all new facts for me, facts that I discovered when I spent time with a prophet today. It made total sense, because I 'know' God's forgiveness, but I often live as if I don't. I fall into the trap of judging myself based on my hip size, because they are way larger than when I worked as a model, but if I am a new creation, I must allow my spirit to challenge this view and look at myself through God's eyes: a challenge, but possible nonetheless.

I laughed out loud today as I realised the full force of my need to avoid myself as I rescue others. I want to be an overcomer. Not only that, I want to be seen to be one too.

I wish there was a humble pill I could take to shortcut this journey, but there isn't. I have to go through the journey. I suppose that even wanting a shortcut shows a lack of humility. I have such a long way to go.

But God.

God is not one to leave us alone for long. Sometimes He does let us flounder for a while in our own mistakes, but not for long.

So today I was woken by God at 6.00 am, and this time I read His word and once more He spoke directly into the heart of the situation and also reminded me that I have been here before.

This is what the Lord says:
'Cursed is the one who trusts in man and who draws strength from mere flesh and whose heart turns away from the Lord. That person will be like a bush in the wastelands; they will not see prosperity when it comes.
They will dwell in the parched places of the desert, in a salt land where no one lives.
'But blessed is the one who trusts in the Lord, whose confidence is in him. They will be like a tree planted by the water that sends out its roots by the stream. It does not fear when the heat comes; its leaves are always green. It has no worries in a year of drought and never fails to bear fruit.'
Jeremiah 17:5–8

Oh my goodness. God spoke straight into the core of my being as He challenged me about claiming back my space: the space alone without my family, the room in my garden that I had abandoned for counselling, almost as if the trauma that was voiced filled the space entirely, leaving no room for me and God. My husband had already suggested to me that I was using it as a place to retreat from the family, but, as you know, I need God to tell me things first! Now I sit in my counselling room, new netbook on my lap, aware of God in this space. I had abandoned this once holy space and now was claiming it back and allowing the wisdom that I share with others to speak into my life as well!

I was diagnosed with arthritis a few months ago in my other hip, and now it needs to be replaced too. The other hip may be leaking metal into my bloodstream and might need replacing again. But you know what? I have peace about it all. God is in charge, nothing takes Him by surprise, unlike me.

***

I am now ten weeks post operation, my hip is really good, the other hip is not leaking metal and I am in charge of my body again. I have found a strange joy in going to the gym, which helps me to feel more grounded, especially as I listen to preaching whilst cycling and working up a sweat!

Life for all the 'daughters – and, for that matter, sons – of the King' is a complex thing. As you now know, I am no different from you. The truth is this: we are never too far from the arms of God; we only have to choose to seek His face to experience Him put out His hand of grace.

> Therefore, I urge you, brothers *and sisters,* in view of God's mercy, to offer your bodies as a living sacrifice, holy and pleasing to God – this is your true and proper worship.
> *Romans 12:1 (italics mine)*

We are participants of the Big Story – participants, not observers.

It's for public consumption, my life.

I offer who I am, in whatever way you choose to use me, Lord.

December 2012.

Epilogue

My dad died on 24th January 2013. My sister and I spent a week with him, day and night, caring for him, praying for him, singing over him. The family that he had chosen to walk away from gathered to him.

My journal says the following: Mandy and I do the terrible, last journey caring for him, then our tears flow hot and fast and then we settle. I love him. I don't want him to be alone, so that he can move from company to the multitudes of heaven and see the Lord.

Time has kaleidoscoped into concentrated memories: good ones come and overwhelm the bad. How much time has been lost over the years through pain, anger and recriminations?

At this time we looked into each other's eyes and said, 'I love you', without words. Was I a newborn child the last time I felt his love like that?

My tears fell painfully on his pillow and he, unable to open his eyes, reached up and tenderly wrapped his hand around my face and wiped my tears. I finally had the tenderness that I had craved all my life, and its purity. It has undone the damage of the past.

Dad sleeps on.

He died at 2:21 pm.

Mandy and I held his hands. How terrible; I miss him already.

***

I now must learn to live differently.